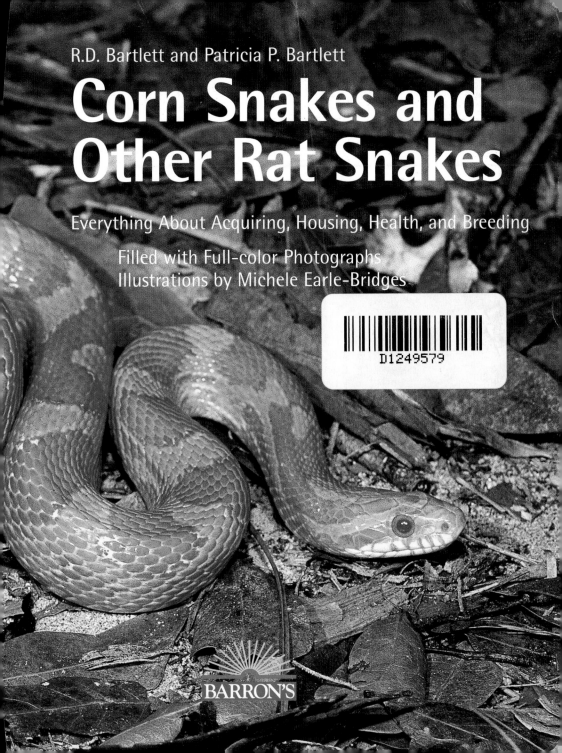

R.D. Bartlett and Patricia P. Bartlett

Corn Snakes and Other Rat Snakes

Everything About Acquiring, Housing, Health, and Breeding

Filled with Full-color Photographs
Illustrations by Michele Earle-Bridges

D1249579

BARRON'S

2 CONTENTS

UNDERSTANDING RAT SNAKES

Rat snakes in general and corn snakes (also called red rat snakes) in particular have become the mainstays of an increasingly reptile-oriented pet industry. At least in name, rat snakes range southward from Palearctic regions to the tropics in both the New and the Old World. The various species are among the world's most popular pet reptiles. Due to their attractive appearance and ready availability, corn snakes are usually a beginning hobbyist's first snake.

The Name

The term "rat snake" is used generically to describe unrelated snakes that feed on rats. However, when used by Americans and Europeans, the term refers to rat-eating constrictors belonging to any of about nine closely related genera.

Rat snakes are fairly easy to find. If you look within the ranges of these snakes to find rodent populations, you are apt to find rat snakes. This is not to say that some specimens will not readily consume baby chicks or occasionally eggs if available, but rat snakes are largely enthusiastic predators of rats.

As shown here, yellow rat snakes can be defensive and, if frightened, will bite.

What Is a Rat Snake?

Compared to the lizards, from which they evolved, snakes are evolutionary newcomers. As best we know, snakes first appeared during the Cretaceous period about 140 million years ago. The serpentine form seems to have been efficient. Certainly, extreme attenuation and narrow girth allow easy access to small areas. In the strictest sense, rat snakes are a terrestrial and arboreal group of colubrine snakes from North and Central America, Europe, and Asia. As we have defined rat snakes in this book, we can add South America and North Africa to the range.

The Basics

Most rat snakes look something like a loaf of bread in cross section—rounded on the top,

This is a very typically colored and patterned Great Plains rat snake.

somewhat flat on the lower sides, and flat on the bottom. The belly scales (or scutes) are angled upward at both sides, which helps in climbing. The scaly skin is dry to the touch; in fact, the scales are formed of intricately folded areas of skin.

TIP

Bites

If you are bitten, don't jerk away as the snake will be unable to disengage its teeth quickly enough to prevent tearing your skin. Your jerking may actually pull the snake's teeth out of its jaw. Give the snake a moment to disengage its teeth, then move away.

The Rat Snake Senses

✔ The "ear" is wholly internal, and consists of a single earbone that is attached to a jawbone, rather than a tympanum. Snakes can hear low-frequency sounds well and they react to ground vibrations with alacrity.

✔ The eye is protected by a brille, a single transparent scale. Snake vision ranges from poor to acute, with the rat snakes being on the higher end of this scale. Motion, by predators or prey is readily perceived.

✔ Both ground and airborne molecules of scent adhere to the extended tongue. The tongue brings the molecules into contact with the sensory Jacobson's organ in the palate, where the scents are sorted out and identified. The analysis is remarkably acute. Two scents that are readily identified are pheromones indi-cating the presence of other snakes and their reproductive readiness, and the presence of food animals.

Breathing

Only the right lung is fully functional. With just a single working lung, respiratory problems in rat snakes are especially serious.

Movement

The forward movement of the rat snake is accomplished by a side-to-side "serpentine movement." The belly scales catch on and push against irregularities in the substrate. The smoother the surface, the harder it is for the snake to crawl across it.

Reproduction

Rat snakes lay eggs (the sole exception being the questionably classified *Oocatochus rufodor-satus*). Depending on the type, eggs from some of the more cold-tolerant species hatch after about two weeks. Eggs from rat snakes in warmer climes may take more than 60 days.

Fertilization is internal. The male fertilizes the female with either one of his two hemipenes.

Behavior

Despite being robust and powerful, these snakes are also secretive, especially by day. They are most apt to be active in the late afternoon, at dusk, and for an hour or two after nightfall. Occasionally, they may wander widely on over-cast days.

The Indonesian rat snake,
Coelognathus subradiatus,
(not discussed) is a popular,
pretty snake.

TIP

An Additional Conservation Note

Remember, genetically mixed snakes should never be released. Humans are doing enough to compromise the efforts of Mother Nature without throwing another variable into the melting pot. Genetic purity must be retained in the wild and it is up to us, as more than casually interested parties, to assure that it is—or that at least our efforts and mistakes do not contribute to its degradation.

Particles of scent are carried into contact with the Jacobson's organ by the flickering tongue of this Trans-Pecos rat snake.

Taxonomy

Until rather recently the rat snakes of the Americas were placed in a single genus, *Elaphe*. However, with new research, and a changing attitude toward taxonomy, the American rat snakes are now split into three genera:

1. *Pantherophis*, the typical rat snakes (including the corn, black, and Baird's rat snakes)

2. *Bogertophis*, the Trans-Pecos and Baja California rat snakes;

3. Senticolis, the green rat snakes.

Availability

Today, snakes are very much a mainstream "pet" and are becoming more so with every passing year. While it is true that many species of snakes are available, a few are captive bred in large numbers. The most popular is the beautiful creature called the corn snake by some and as the red rat snake by others. (We'll use the name corn snake since this is the standardized common name.)

Commonly Kept Species

This book covers rat snakes commonly available in the pet market. We have made no effort to discuss many of the seldom-seen Asian taxa here. Even so, you will note that the lion's share of this coverage has been directed at the many morphs, normal and selectively derived, of the American corn and black rat snake complexes that, together, are probably the most commonly kept and extensively bred of the world's snake species. Although a basic text, we hope that the comments made here will benefit both neophyte and experienced keepers and the snakes they keep.

This corn snake has just finished laying her clutch on a substrate of damp sphagnum moss in the egg-deposition container.

New Versus Old World

Strangely, among the rat snakes of the world, the American rat snakes are also among the easiest to keep and breed. Both of these factors have contributed to their ready availability and inexpensive prices.

Conversely, although we do not yet know exactly why, many of the Old World rat snakes are difficult to keep, not to mention breed. When Old World species are available, either from the wild or as captive-born hatchlings from the small cadre of hobbyists to have succeeded with them, the prices are high.

This is especially true for captive bred babies. The reason for the high-priced babies is their survival factor. They are usually much easier to maintain than wild-collected specimens.

The Ethics and Arguments Regarding Hybridization

As long as simple intergrades and hybrids are produced solely for the pet trade, we see nothing at all wrong with these breeding programs.

When the practice was first begun by herpetoculturists, it was deplored by conservationists and herpetocultural purists alike. Understandably, these two groups remain opposed to the practice. Much of the furor was brought on by the breeders themselves who claimed breeding as a conservation/reintroduction tool.

Remember that intergrades and/or hybrids should never be released into the wild, no matter how depleted wild stocks actually do become; thus, neither intergrades nor hybrids could ever be anything but pet trade specimens. The only conservation value from them is that their availability may reduce pet trade collecting of wild specimens. It would have been more acceptable if the hobbyists (the vast majority of whom will never be involved with any serious conservation program) had simply said, "We are now producing serpentine 'mutts' for the pet industry. This effort is a money-maker for us, and the conservation aspects, if any, are simply that purchasers of our snakes will not be drawing as heavily on wild populations and will, hopefully, be learning respect for a beleaguered group of animals." The conservationists and purists would still have been alarmed, but one argument against the practice would have been largely defused.

So, if we don't breed snakes for conservation, why do we breed them? Because we want to, because we enjoy them, because we can learn from them!

A portrait of a twin-spotted rat snake.

Rat Snake Colors and Patterns

Throughout the world, the patterns and colors of rat snakes repeat themselves over and over. The hatchlings and juveniles of many are prominently blotched and, as growth occurs, the blotches fade and may be replaced by longitudinal striping.

Many widely separated species are remarkably similar in external appearance; for example, the pretty saddled pattern of the American corn snake, *Pantherophis guttatus*, is echoed in the European leopard snake, *Zamenis situla*, as well as in the Latin American *Pseudoelaphe flavirufa*, and the Transcaucasian rat snake, *Z. hohenackeri*, and, to a lesser degree, in the Chinese red-headed rat snake, *Orthriophis moellendorfi*. The striping of several of the

The blotched hatchlings of the Everglades rat snakes are pale in color.

*A yellow rat snake (top) coils
with an Everglades rat snake.*

European rat snakes (*E. quatuorlineata* and
Rhinechis scalaris among them) is quite reminiscent of the striping seen on the American
yellow rat snake, *P. obsoletus quadrivittata* and
the Japanese *E. quadrivirgata.*

Defenses/Offenses

Teeth

Everyone knows that snakes bite. Even the
most innocuous of the nonvenomous species
can and will bite if threatened. Rat snakes are
certainly no exception and even those captive
bred and hatched for many generations will
occasionally bite.

All rat snakes have small teeth that are
arranged in several rows (four in the upper
jaw, two in the lower), and are slightly curved,
which is designed to prevent the escape of prey
items once grasped. Snakes don't chew their
food; they overpower it and swallow it whole.

You will soon learn the best method of avoid-
ing injury is to avoid bites. It won't take a lot of
observation on your part to determine when and
whether your rat snake is upset. If it is, either
leave it alone or handle it carefully with a snake
hook. If you are bitten, remove any teeth that
may remain in the wound, wash the bite carefully, and administer an antiseptic/antibacterial
agent. A bandage will remind you to be more
careful and elicit sympathy from your friends—
unless they keep snakes as well.

Muscles

If restrained (especially near the head or
neck) the snake will coil tightly around the
restraining object and try to pull free. The
amount of strength possessed by the snake
is remarkable.

Musking

If restrained, rat snakes will smear the con-
tents of the anal glands and intestinal tract on
their captor. This is called "musking." It is odorif-
erous and disconcerting, but not of serious con-
sequence. Although this admonition is probably
entirely unnecessary, wash carefully if smeared.

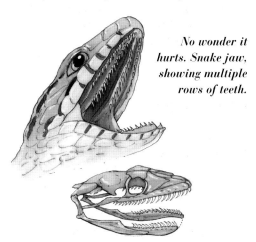

*No wonder it
hurts. Snake jaw,
showing multiple
rows of teeth.*

ACQUIRING YOUR RAT SNAKE

To succeed with rat snakes, you first must acquire healthy examples from reputable sources. In many cases, this will involve shipping from distant regions. Paying careful attention to details can spare you from costly mistakes.

Choosing a Healthy Rat Snake

Keeping a rat snake in captivity over a long period of time is a lot easier if you start with a healthy snake. Actually determining the state of health of a potential purchase may be somewhat difficult to do because, like all reptiles, rat snakes may behave normally—show no outward signs of ill health—until they are seriously ill. But there are a few clues to look for when choosing a pet rat snake, or a snake of any species.

Basic Behavior

Rat snakes are often secretive, surviving by staying out of the way of possible predators, and remaining beneath cover for long periods. Rat snakes tend to be "wait-and-ambush"

This is a hypomelanistic adult Everglades rat snake.

predators; they simply wait until prey happens along in front of them. Arboreal types may remain quietly sprawled along a sturdy limb or leaning trunk. This quiet demeanor may make them seem less than alert, but actually nothing could be further from the truth.

Note: Until you become entirely familiar with rat snakes and their normal behavior, take a knowledgeable person with you when you go to pick one out. Select a snake that displays an alert demeanor when disturbed. Keep in mind that some species are naturally more belligerent than others. Corn snakes, for example, are fairly calm rat snakes. In addition to looking for a calm snake, if you're a beginner, choose one of the hardier types of rat snakes.

Does It Eat?

When selecting your snake, look at its general appearance. Check the overall size and body weight. Although some species are

A snow white leucistic strain of the Texas rat snake is readily available in the pet trade.

normally more slender than others, a lengthwise skin fold along the sides or "accordion" ribs is a caution sign. Ask the dealer, private or commercial, about the snake. Ask if the specimen is feeding and watch it feed, if possible, even for something as commonplace as a corn snake hatchling. Some corn snakes never feed after emerging from the egg; no one knows why.

Sneezing

Ask if the snake is sneezing. A snake that is sneezing may have a respiratory infection; labored breathing may mean that lung flukes are present. Both of these problems are hard to diagnose in a living snake and postmortem diagnosis is frustrating for you and pointless for that snake.

Will It Bite?

Ask if the snake can be handled. A snake that does not strike wildly at an approaching hand will be easier for you to take care of once you get it home.

The Commitment

If given good care, many rat snakes are wonderful and long-lived pets. It is not unusual for a rat snake of any type to live more than ten years in captivity. If you choose your specimen(s) carefully, the chances are good that you will become a satisfied hobbyist.

Handling: Dos and Don'ts

Use a hook: Although many rat snakes do not object to gentle handling, others may never adjust to it. This is especially true of many of the Asian rat snake species, some of which not only wriggle wildly when held, but bite indiscriminately. Consider these snakes display animals only—animals to be watched and appreciated, lifted, moved, and manipulated on a snake hook, but not handled.

Use a box: Add a cardboard or plastic hiding box to the cage. Many specimens will remain quietly in their hidebox. If the hidebox has a secure bottom, hidebox and all can be

A deep red ground color with almost no visible pattern typifies the adult blood-red corn snake.

lifted and moved without disturbing the snake.

Be gentle: When you do hold a rat snake, remember that even a rather small specimen can and will bite if the snake is carelessly restrained. Even such relatively easy-to-handle specimens as corn snakes and yellow rat snakes do not like to be suddenly grasped. Handle all specimens gently; do not tap on the terrarium glass or cage front, and, if your specimen displays reluctance at being lifted, manipulate it first with a hook.

Even if your snake bites you, do not drop it. A drop can result in damage to its internal organs or broken bones. Although arboreal species may be a little more accustomed to an occasional fall, they still should never be handled carelessly.

Location Matters

The hobby of keeping reptiles is, of course, not limited to any one section of the United States, Europe, or Asia; however, the availability of reptiles is, unquestionably, better in some regions of those countries than in others.

Like this tropical rat snake (Spilotes pullatus), many rat snakes inflate their throats vertically when frightened.

Many wild-collected, nervous rat snakes abrade their nose during shipping. This is a red-tailed green rat snake.

Dealers

In the United States, the largest reptile dealers are located in California, Florida, and New York. Reptiles are shipped by air freight from the larger cities in these states to wholesalers in other cities who, in turn, supply pet shops and, in some cases, herpetocultural breeders. There is usually some overlap among these businesses.

Pet Shops

Although most pet shops can provide good information on the animals they sell, some rely on information given to them by their distributors/suppliers. Unfortunately, information given, even inaccurate information, is often self-perpetuating.

There are some facts that your shop cannot reasonably be expected to know. Among these are the origin of a given wild-collected speci-

Shipping

Door-to-door deliveries of reptiles and amphibians, as well as airport-to-airport services are available. Shipping is not inexpensive, but it is fast and usually very reliable. It is best to avoid shipping herps during very hot or very cold weather, or during high-travel holiday seasons. Unless you know your dealer well, it will usually be necessary to pay for the herp and shipping in advance.

Many dealers insist on cashier's checks, money orders, credit cards, or payment by Pay Pal. Do not hesitate to ask your dealer about the method of payment required as well as about what means or company the animal will be shipped by, which level of service will be used, estimated cost (including packing and handling), and the dealer's stance on dead animals in case an unfortunate accident does occur. Many dealers will guarantee live arrival if you work within their guidelines.

men and the genetics of either normal-appearing or aberrant specimens that are captive bred. Remember, your local pet shop is often two or even three or four times removed from the source of the specimen.

Specialty Dealers

The continuing growth in popularity of reptiles has created the specialty dealers. Specialty dealers may breed reptiles themselves and also

Many wild-collected rat snakes, such as this yellow-striped rat snake (Coelognathus flavolineatus), *arrive in the pet trade seriously dehydrated and are then difficult to acclimate.*

deal directly with other breeders worldwide; they are often better able to answer your questions. Their imported specimens are usually acclimated, have been fed, and have often been subjected to a veterinary checkup. It is from the specialty dealers that the broadest selection of the world's rat snakes is usually available.

Breeders

Breeders, whether specialist hobbyists or commercial breeders, are probably the best sources of parasite-free, well-acclimated specimens and accurate information. Most breeders keep records of genetics, lineage, fecundity, health, and the quirks of the specimens with which they work. These records are invariably available to their customers.

Changes in appearance: Keep in mind that most rat snake species change color and/or pattern (some dramatically so) throughout their long lives. Some are blotched and pale as babies, and striped and richly colored as adults; others may just be paler diminutives of the adults. While a breeder or dealer may well know what the adult breeder rat snakes look like, it is impossible to guarantee that all offspring will be identical to each other. After all, you don't look exactly like your parents. Reputable dealers and breeders will do anything possible to provide you with the finest quality stock, but, despite all your purveyor's efforts, at adulthood your snake may end up being duller or brighter than its parents—or even very like them. Be prepared for all eventualities.

YOUR RAT SNAKE'S HEALTH

Once acclimated, your rat snake should experience few health problems if kept properly. However, it is always better to find a reptile-oriented veterinarian before one is actually needed.

Shedding

The age and health of your rat snake will have much to do with the frequency with which it sheds its skin. A healthy, fast-growing baby will shed its skin several times a year, much more frequently than a slowly growing adult or an ill specimen.

A specimen suffering from a mite infestation or from a malady known as blister disease (see page 24), may enter a rapid shed cycle in an effort to correct the problem. If the irritation factor is corrected (the mites eliminated or the cage cleaned and dried), skin defects caused by the disease will often disappear after two or three sheds. Adult rat snakes will shed their skin soon after emerging from hibernation (or brumation—the terms are basically interchangeable).

Gonyosoma frenatus is rather closely allied to the Asian red-tailed green rat snake.

Following this springtime shed, most rat snakes are ready for breeding. Gravid females will shed again prior to egg deposition. The shedding process (also called molting or, more properly, ecdysis) results from thyroid activity. A week or so prior to shedding, as the old skin begins to loosen from the new one forming beneath it, your rat snake's skin may dull and take on an overall grayish or silvery sheen. The snake's eyes will temporarily look bluish. A snake in this phase is colloquially referred to as blue or opaque by hobbyists.

A snake that is blue may be more irritable during this time, which can be due to systemic changes or simply because it cannot see as well and therefore feels more easily threatened. After shedding, your specimen will again be as brightly hued and patterned as it was to begin with.

Snakes in the wild seldom have problems shedding, but some captives may. The problem may be due to the stress experienced by a new

Eastern fox snakes are attractive but may be difficult to induce to feed if imprinted on wild prey species.

import, dehydration, starvation, or when the relative humidity in the terrarium or cage is too low.

How Shedding Is Accomplished

Generally speaking, the snake simply rubs its nose against a rock or limb in its cage to loosen the skin, then catches the edge of the skin against the rock or limb and crawls out of the old skin. It is important that no patches of old skin remain attached to the snake. If the snake seems to have difficulty in the shedding process, place it in a damp cloth bag overnight and make sure temperatures are regulated. This usually loosens the old skin and allows your snake to shed. Occasionally, you may have to manually help your snake rid itself of a reluctant shed.

Starting with a Healthy Snake

Before acquiring your rat snake—or any reptile or amphibian—locate a veterinarian who is familiar with, has the ability, and is willing to treat these creatures. Believe us when we say that not every veterinarian is qualified or willing. Find your reptile veterinarian by inquiring at your local pet store, or going online to the Web site of the Association of Reptile and Amphibian Veterinarians.

As always, the starting point for assuring the good health of your herps begins with the basics. Start with healthy examples. Purchase your herp from a reliable supplier, but only after asking many pertinent questions such as whether it was captive bred or wild collected, if it is feeding well, and if so, on what, and whether a fecal exam for endoparasites has been performed. These questions are especially pertinent if you are considering the purchase of any rat snake collected from the wild or intend to acquire a difficult-to-acclimate species such as the Moellendorff's or the Mandarin rat snake.

If you are planning an on-line, mail-order purchase, it is not always possible to actually see the rat snake in which you are interested, but the dealer/breeder can post a high resolution picture (jpg or tiff) of the actual creature. Although it is better to purchase a captive-bred or -born herp than a wild-collected one, this is not always possible.

Once ascertaining as fully as possible that the rat snake in question is in good health and actually the one you wish to acquire, assess your facilities. The cage you are providing must be both escape-proof and suitable in every aspect to the well-being of the inhabitant.

✔ The cage must provide sufficient space, adequate humidity (or lack of same), and a suitable temperature regime.

✔ You must be able to provide a supply of fresh water and suitable food.

✔ Proper cage temperature and relative humidity are very important factors. All facets of proper caging for the species involved must be addressed.

Even with the best of care, health problems and concerns may occur. If caught in time, some health problems respond well to treatment, but others are irreversible, eventually fatal, and may be extremely communicable to other reptiles or amphibians. Prevention is invariably better than cure.

Quarantine

Isolation of a newly acquired or ailing specimen is very important. Your quarantine facilities should be in an area well separated from other specimens and the quarantine period should be for no fewer than 30 days (60 to 90 days is better).

The quarantine cage should be as sterile as possible, yet still appointed suitably to provide for the comfort of the animal. If more than one rat snake is acquired, each should be housed individually during this period. After working with your quarantined snake, wash your hands and arms thoroughly before working with other snakes.

During this period, observe your new pet for any signs of respiratory distress or other symptoms of adverse health. Discuss your findings with your veterinarian, if applicable. This is, of course, an excellent time to have fresh fecal samples tested for endoparasites.

Health Problems

Parasites

External parasites are typically ticks and mites. Both plague reptiles; getting rid of them can be bothersome but is very important. Ticks are usually present only on imported snakes and are readily visible. Snake mites may be present

Ticks, like this one on the tail tip of a Trans-Pecos rat snake, should be promptly and carefully removed.

on both imported and captive-born snakes, and their much smaller size makes them hard to see.

Mites are very easily transported from vendor to vendor and cage to cage. If infested with mites, your uncomfortable snake will often rub its face and body along a shelf or perch, twitch, or soak incessantly in its water bowl. The belly scales may be puffed out and ooze serum.

Both ticks and mites have been implicated in the transmission of serious, often fatal diseases such as inclusion body disease, which affects the central nervous system and is thought to be transmitted by endoparasites and by snake-to-snake contact.

There are several ways to rid your snakes of these pests. You can use a pair of plastic tweezers especially made for removing ticks, available at your pet store or from your veterinarian, to literally twist them off the snake. Both mites and ticks can be eliminated via airborne insecticides such as "No-pest Strips" (today's formula does not seem to be as reliable as the original) or by desiccating the pests with Sevin or DryDie (desiccants are best used in low-humidity situations), or by spraying the snake and its enclosure with dilute Ivermectin (don't use Ivermectin near or on amphibians—it will be fatal).

Note: Although there are several commercially prepared mite eradication products now available, the authors have had no practical experience with any of them.

Ivermectin is easily administered from a spray bottle. Put the snake in a holding cage and moving slowly, gently spray the snake. Administer the spray sparingly near the snake's head.

Cleaning the cage: While the snake is in the holding cage, clean its home cage and any cage furniture thoroughly.

✔ Wash all nooks and crannies and cage furnishings with a dilute Ivermectin or dilute bleach solution.

✔ Rinse the cage and furnishings thoroughly and let them air-dry before reintroducing the snake to the cage.

✔ Be sure to wash and disinfect the holding cage in which the snake was placed while its permanent cage was being cleaned.

✔ Since treatments destroy only the mites themselves and leave their eggs still viable, it will be necessary to treat the snakes at least twice at nine-day intervals to kill hatching mites.

Internal parasites or endoparasites: These parasites, such as cestodes and/or protozoa, may be present. All are easily eradicated, but all do not respond to the same treatment. We suggest that you consult your veterinarian for diagnosis and treatment if you suspect there may be an internal parasite problem. Administering medications orally will require physically restraining the snake, which may take two sets of hands.

Protozoans called Cryptosporidium ssp.: These are almost omnipresent, but seldom cause healthy reptiles distress. However, if the snake is stressed or its immune system is already fighting another pathogen, cryptosporidia may proliferate and cause a chronic and often fatal inability to digest food fully. If your snake begins to regurgitate frequently, seek veterinary assessment.

Trauma (Burns, Bites, and Injuries)

Burns: The problem of thermal burns from a malfunctioning hot rock or improperly baffled bulb or ceramic heater is one that should never occur. These sort of injuries are absolutely preventable on your part.

Juvenile Baird's rat snakes, **Pantherophis bairdi,** *have a busy pattern of dorsal blotches.*

The primitive nervous system of reptiles and amphibians may allow these creatures to rest against a nonshielded light bulb or an over-heating hot rock, even while burning themselves severely. Carefully shield all exposed light bulbs or ceramic heating units with a wire net or cage, taking care that there are no sharp edges on which the cage inhabitant can injure itself. Rather than hot rocks, use thermostatically controlled under-terrarium heaters to elevate cage temperatures for reptiles. If a reptile sustains a burn, the injury should be dressed with an antibacterial burn ointment.

Bites: Despite the fact that most rat snakes will readily accept prekilled mice, many keepers choose to feed their reptiles live mice or rats. A bite by an adult rodent can be very serious.

Although it is true that snakes are predators that usually successfully overcome their prey with no incident, this is not always the case. Prey animals have been known to seriously injure reptiles in whose cages they have been left. Reptiles will often not make any effort to overcome an aggressive prey animal. The reptile may even refuse that particular kind of prey in the future. If bitten in the eye by a rodent, blindness may result. Mouth rot (infectious stomatitis) may develop from a bite or a scratch to the gums or mouth interior. Gaping wounds have been chewed into the sides of reptiles by an unmonitored rodent.

We urge that all prey animals be prekilled or, if for some reason they are not, that prey can never be left unwatched in your reptile's cage.

If your reptile is seriously bitten, a dressing of the wound with antibacterial powder may be necessary. Immediately seek veterinary assessment.

Injuries: Injuries may occasionally occur if your rat snake sustains a fall or is dropped while being carried. Spinal injuries are serious and each must be individually assessed. Some may necessitate that the snake be euthanized. Support your rat snake while it is being carried, and if it uses a favored elevated basking site, be sure that a yielding substrate is in the cage.

A broken or injured tail may occasionally occur. This can happen through an accident such as your rat snake getting caught beneath or between improperly stabilized cage furniture, getting caught in the cage door, or through a more natural cause such as the skin not being fully shed from the tail. Both causes are easily avoided. Be sure all cage furniture, especially heavy rocks or climbing limbs, are properly affixed. Be sure your rat snake is entirely in the cage before closing the cage door. And be certain that with each shed all fragments of skin are removed. If a portion of the skin is left on the tail, moisten it with water, mineral oil, or a commercial skin-shedding agent and remove it manually.

Mouth rot (infectious stomatitis). This condition can occur if a reptile's teeth or jaw are broken or its mouth lining is injured (by a rodent bite or other trauma such as striking at the side of its cage). The medication of choice may be Neosporin or a liquid sulfa drug. We have found hydrogen peroxide, sulfamethazine, and sulfathiazole sodium to be effective. If advanced to the stage where the snake's jawbones are affected and its teeth are loosened, veterinary assistance should be sought. This is a disfiguring disease that can be fatal if not treated. Acclimate your pet reptile to eating prekilled rodents, house it correctly, and do not withdraw sharply (breaking its teeth) if you happen to be bitten.

Respiratory ailments may plague a reptile maintained improperly or otherwise stressed. Respiratory distress is especially apt to occur when the cage humidity is high, the cage is damp, and temperatures are suboptimal. Arid-land rat snakes being kept in an area of high humidity are particularly susceptible. Not all cases respond to the same antibiotic. Sensitivity tests must be made. Untreated respiratory ailments can quickly become debilitating and, if unchecked, eventually fatal. Seek veterinary assessment and help.

Bacterial, Fungal, and Viral Diseases

Vesicular dermatitis (blister disease syndrome): This is evidenced when a snake's skin bears many tiny white blister-appearing lesions. The causative agents for blistering can be many and the malady, which can ultimately be fatal, can be difficult to cure if not treated early.

Blistering can result from keeping a snake in a dirty, wet cage. Prolonged soaking in the water bowl may also cause blistering.

If a reptile persists in soaking, first check the animals for the presence of mites (treat immediately if found), then replace the bowl with a smaller one.

Keep cage temperatures optimal. Prevent excessive humidity by providing adequate air flow and cage ventilation. Keep the substrate dry and clean.

Should vesicular dermatitis occur, immediately assess and correct your regimen of husbandry and seek the help of a reptile-oriented veterinarian. If the serum-containing blisters are numerous or if skin damage is apparent, lesions may already be present on internal organs. Sensitivity tests are necessary, and antibiotic treatment will necessarily be lengthy.

Paramyxovirus: This is a very communicable, insidious, and eventually fatal viral disease of some snake species. As it advances it causes spasms, loss of neuromotor control (especially noticeable in uncoordinated head motions), gaping, wheezing, and bloody mucus in the mouth. It has no known cure. This disease is highly contagious. The snake should be humanely euthanized. Know your supplier and quarantine all incoming snakes. Consult your veterinarian immediately.

Popeye: This occurs in snakes when the space between the eye and the brille becomes filled with discolored serum. The cause could be infection (often *Pseudomonas*), injury of the eye or related ducts, or other causes. Blindness or loss of the eye may result. Consult a veterinarian promptly.

Egg retention (dystocia): Occasionally, if husbandry conditions are not exactly correct, if the female's health is marginal, or if an egg is misshapen, a rat snake may retain one or more eggs from a clutch. It is imperative that the retained eggs are removed. Because the oviducts are so fragile, help from a reptile-oriented veterinarian should be sought.

Regurgitation syndrome: Regurgitation can result from a number of causes. Among other things, the eating of an oversized prey item, dehydration, endoparasites, improper cage humidity, or temperature fluctuations can cause nonassimilation of the food and result in regurgitation.

The regurgitation of a meal is stressful on any snake but is especially so if the snake is not in top-notch condition. Everything possible should be done to assure that regurgitation does not occur.

Protect against regurgitation by these measures:

1. Ascertain that the terrarium is always maintained at a temperature suitable for the snake.

2. Do not allow sharp fluctuations of terrarium temperature. Monitor and control day/night temperature changes and against the fluctuations that might occur during the passage of a strong cold front.

3. Monitor and control cage humidity. This is especially important to the well-being of arid-land rat snakes.

4. Make sure that your rat snake is not overburdened with endoparasites.

5. Be certain that your rat snake is properly hydrated. Some new imports (especially arboreal rat snake species) may not recognize drinking water in a dish. Until acclimated, these snakes may require frequent misting or need the water in the dish to be roiled by an airstone.

6. Feed suitably sized prey. The prey animal should not be significantly larger than the snake's head.

7. If your snake does regurgitate, clean and sterilize its cage, check all of the variables mentioned above and wait a few days before feeding it a very small meal.

By properly controlling the initial health and terrarium conditions of your rat snake, you can minimize the chances of digestion problems. However, if all of the listed criteria are addressed and corrected, and if your snake continues to regurgitate, veterinary assessment (and, if needed, intervention) should be sought.

CAGING YOUR RAT SNAKE

Whether the rat snake species you choose is terrestrial or arboreal, and whether it is a denizen of arid lands or wet savannas will make a difference in how it is caged. How much time you want to spend on cage maintenance will determine what furnishings to add.

Choosing a Tank

These general descriptions pertain to housing for most of the "easier" rat snake species and subspecies. Among these are various subspecies of corn, black, and Baird's rat snakes (*P. guttatus* ssp., *P. obsoletus* ssp., and *P. bairdi*, respectively), many of the beauty or striped-tailed rat snakes, *O. taeniurus* ssp., and other species of similar size. For some of the more difficult species, see the species accounts in this book (beginning on page 87).

Today, buying caging for snakes is as easy as going to your local pet store, where cages made specifically for snakes are available, as well as aquarium tanks that may be converted into perfectly acceptable reptile terraria.

This is a pretty corn snake from north central Florida.

Choosing the basic tank is an easy procedure—the difficult part will be deciding how elaborate you want the cage to be, which is directly related to how much time you want to spend on cage maintenance.

Simple "American-Style" Caging

Over the years, American herpetoculturists have become known for caging snakes in the simplest, most utilitarian manner possible. American hobbyists usually opt for the bare minimum when setting up a cage. Many hobbyists begin with an empty aquarium tank or plastic shoebox and add little more than an absorbent bottom of folded newspaper, paper towels or aspen shavings, an untippable water bowl, and a hidebox. The hardier rat snakes species seem to thrive, and some, such as corn snakes, will even breed, in such Spartan quarters.

Vertically oriented cages are preferred for arboreal rat snakes.

✔ If plastic caging is used, sufficient ventilation holes must be drilled or melted through the sides to provide adequate air transfer and to prevent excessive humidity from building up within. Ventilation holes should on at least two sides—often on all four sides. If an arid climate rat snake is being kept, ventilate the top as well.

✔ Shelving systems that hold a dozen or more plastic boxes are now available, many with heat tapes built in. These are advertised in most reptile magazines and at many of the reptile meets.

✔ Glass aquaria can be oriented in either a normal horizontal or a vertical position, as desired. If you opt for a vertical orientation, the clip-on screen top can serve as a side. Glue feet on the side of the tank serving as the bottom so the top is easy to take off and put on. If you prefer, you can construct a vertical system from two tanks of the same size. After accidentally breaking the bottom of what had been a standard 15-gallon (56.7-L) tank, and then placing that tank on top of another, we found we could easily "construct" vertically oriented terraria that are ideal for arboreal rat snakes.

✔ Custom glass terraria can either be purchased or, if you are just the slightest bit handy, can be built by you. Merely take your measurements, cut the pieces of glass or have them cut, and using a latex aquarium sealant, build your custom tank. The glass can be held in place with strips of tape while the sealant cures in about 24 hours. The most important thing when using the latex is to make absolutely certain that the edges of the glass that are to be sealed are completely free of any oils or any other debris that could prevent the aquarium sealant

Requirements

✔ Plastic shoe, sweater, and blanket boxes are available in many hardware and department stores. Be sure the lids fit securely, or can be secured with tape or Velcro strips. Aquarium tanks, of course, are available in virtually any pet department and screen lids are a standard stock item.

from forming a tight seal. Remarkably large terraria can be held together very securely with aquarium sealant, especially if the tanks will not be used to hold water.

"European-Style" Caging

In direct contrast to the starkness preferred by most American hobbyists, the Europeans have become well known for the intricacy of detail that goes into the construction of their terrarium interiors. They prefer to reconstruct a little corner of nature, a working, miniaturized ecosystem, in their terraria. This concept has stood the Europeans in good stead, for several rat snake species considered difficult to impossible by most American hobbyists are rather routinely bred by continental herpetoculturists. The European concept is to fit the terrarium setting to the species in question.

Pros: In reality, both the American and European concepts have their places. It is far easier to care for large numbers of specimens in the rather sterile, generic American-type cages than in the intricate terraria of the European hobbyists.

Cons: To successfully create a terrarium in the European style takes knowledge, time, and dedication—you do not need only an understanding of your rat snakes, but an understanding of the dynamics of their habitat as well. You then must recreate that habitat in the cage, and keep it viable. It is not an easy task.

Additionally, although a natural setting is more conducive to normal behavior by the snakes, a cage like this may actually be more difficult to maintain than one that is less intricate. If the naturalistic terrarium is too damp, too dry, or has incorrect lighting, not only will the vegetation suffer, but so can the serpentine inhabitants.

Inside the Cage

Cage Furniture

Many rat snakes are climbers, especially within the confines of captivity. However, climbing requires the firm stability provided by sizable limbs, not the uncertainty of pliant twigs. Tree limbs need to be at least one and a half times the diameter of the snake.

Limbs, cut to the exact inside length of the terrarium, can be secured at any level with thick U-shaped beads of aquarium sealant that have been placed on the aquarium glass. Merely slide the limb downward into the open top of the U until the limb rests securely in place.

Other cage furniture, whether naturalistic or "plastic functional," can be used.

Hiding

Rat snakes enjoy—and some need—hiding areas for seclusion and security. This is especially true if the cage is located in a heavily trafficked area and the inhabitant is a nervous species.

✔ Preformed plastic caves are readily available at many pet and reptile dealers. These are washable and can be sterilized, and will last for years.

✔ Parakeet and cockatiel nesting boxes are readily accepted by most species of rat snakes.

✔ A disposable cardboard box, such as a shoebox, with an access hole cut in one end will also provide shelter.

✔ We provide natural-looking hollow limbs that we pick up as we find them in woods and fields. These can be used as floor furnishings or can be glued into place with aquarium sealant at suitable levels.

✔ Corkbark is a reasonable alternative to the hollow limbs and is much lighter, more impervious to body wastes, and easily cleaned and

Eastern fox snakes, **Pantherophis gloydi,** *use all types of debris for hiding. This adult was found in a discarded carpet.*

sterilized for lengthy use. It is available at many pet stores, reptile dealers, and plant nurseries.

Lighting, Heating, and Weather Patterns

Staying Warm

Snakes, being ectothermic—the old term was cold-blooded—creatures, regulate their body temperature by utilizing outside sources of heating and cooling.

At most times, they warm themselves by basking in a secluded yet sunny place.

When they are preparing to shed and vision is impaired, they are more secretive and seek warmed areas beneath litter—discarded sheets of plywood and rusted roofing tin are two favored examples—or under natural cover such as flat rocks. In areas with rocky ledges or hollowed fallen trees, the snakes may merely rest in the entryway of their denning area and extend a coil or two of body out into the sun.

While tropical and semitropical rat snakes may remain active the year round, northern snakes hibernate (brumate). Snakes in areas that are subject to only periodic cold spells may become dormant only during those cold spells. Even though semiactive, these snakes may not feed for most of the cooler time of the year.

Staying Cool

Although different snake species have adapted to different environments, it is important for snakes to remain comfortable. During hot weather, or where temperatures are naturally very hot, rat snakes are either nocturnal or may aestivate (undergo a period of warm-weather dormancy) through the weeks of excessive heat.

Weather and Behavior

Naturally changing weather patterns—dry seasons, rainy seasons, low-pressure frontal systems, the high pressure associated with fine weather, and even the lunar cycle—are known to affect snake behavior. Rat snakes are often most active during the dark of the moon, during unsettled weather, and at the changing of the tropical seasons (from wet to dry or, more common, vice versa).

Reproductive behavior is often stimulated by the lowering barometric pressures that occur at the advent of a storm, and the increase in humidity.

Natural light cycles are nearly as important to the snakes as temperature. Under normal conditions, snake activity is greatest during the

Rat snakes (like this yellow rat snake) often hide in tree hollows.

longest days of the year (which coincide with the most optimum temperatures as well). Those snakes that hibernate do so during the shortest days of the year.

Thermoregulation: This is important even for captive snakes. They, of course, are then dependent on us, their keepers, to provide them with caging that permits them to select their body temperature. Warming the cage can be done with heating pads, heating tapes, and hot rocks, although the latter are not particularly recommended.

Ceramic heating units: These units, which screw into a light socket, and light bulbs, especially those with directed beams such as flood and spotlights, are other possible sources of heat, and the bulbs provide light as well as heat.

Fluorescent bulbs: These will provide light but little heat, which can be advantageous when you live in a warmer area where not much additional heat is needed.

Temperature: Provide thermal gradients except during hibernation when the terrarium temperature should be uniformly cool (see the species account for *Senticolis triaspis intermedia*, page 80, for what may be the sole exception to this statement). For nonhibernation temperatures, keep one end of the tank cool (preferably 65–75°F [18–24°C]) and provide heat at the other end. The warm end of the tank can be between 75–82°F (24–28°C) for rat snakes from high altitude or northern climes, to as high as 88–95°F (31–35°C) for warmth-loving species. See the species accounts, beginning on page 54, for specific temperature suggestions. In small tanks, we put the hide box on the cool end of the tank. If the tank is sufficiently large, we put a hide box on both ends.

Caution: Make certain that whatever heating unit you choose is thermostatically controlled. Please note that, while the current type of heat rocks is more reliable than its predecessors,

A portrait of a Trans-Pecos rat snake.

serious thermal burns have occurred during use. If you use a heat rock, monitor it carefully.

Full-Spectrum/Ultraviolet Light

We are often asked whether we feel ultraviolet illumination is necessary for rat snakes. It doesn't seem to be necessary for reptiles that consume whole warm-blooded prey; the animals seem to get all their vitamin D and calcium needs met by this diet. For amphibians and reptiles that consume only insects, full-spectrum lighting and supplementary calcium is needed. Because our caging area may contain a mix of reptiles and amphibians, we provide full-spectrum lighting above each caging shelf.

While the amount of UV supplied may be negligible, the color-temperature of full-spectrum bulbs—a means by which the amount of

natural sunlight-like light is measured—may be beneficial to captive snakes.

Rather than heat/cool/light individual cages, some very successful hobbyists group species with similar needs (even if individually caged) and treat them as a single unit. The temperature of the entire room is thermostatically controlled. Lighting is controlled to yield a natural/normal photoperiod (usually 16 hours of daylight in the summer and 10 hours of daylight in the winter—check the sunrise/sunset times in your daily paper for seasonal shifts). This means that the room/cage is illuminated during the daylight hours and darkened at night. While this is effective for most of the easily kept, nondemanding rat snakes, it seems less satisfactory for many of the more specialized European and Asiatic species. Montane and

This is a typical appearing Trans-Pecos rat snake.

lowland species differ in their high and low temperature requirements.

Water, Soaking Bowls, and Cage Humidity

Although the several arid climate (desert and savanna) forms of rat snakes may drink and soak less often than the more humidity-tolerant "typical" species, water is critical for all. Cage humidity can be an important consideration in successful maintenance. Species from humid areas will have shedding problems if the humidity is too low; species from desert areas can develop serious, even fatal, health problems if humidity is too high. In the latter case, hobbyists have found that species such as Trans-Pecos and Baja California rat snakes—two of the most aridland-dwelling species—may languish if kept in the perpetual high humidity of our southeastern coastal plain states.

Besides serving as a drinking receptacle, the water bowl can play an integral part in raising or lowering the humidity in a cage. Cage humidity will be higher in a cage lacking adequate ventilation than in one with more adequate air circulation.

If you wish to increase, then retain, a high humidity in your cage, place the water bowl in the hottest spot (over a heating pad if one is being used). If you wish to decrease, or keep humidity as low as possible, place the water bowl in the coolest spot in the cage.

Please note: If your snake is opaque or blue, the condition assumed prior to skin-shedding, you may wish to have a water dish large enough for your snake to soak in the cage at all times. Also, snakes often prowl actively when they are thirsty. If your snake seems excessively active, check its water bowl to make sure water is available. If it is a desert species and you have limited access to a water bowl, allow the snake to have a water bowl for an hour or so.

The Mexican night snake, **Pseudelaphe flavirufa pardalina,** *is a corn snake look-alike from south of the border.*

FEEDING YOUR RAT SNAKE

Although in the wild rat snakes often prey upon live rodents, prekilled prey is usually the best choice for captive snakes. If live prey is given, you must carefully watch that your snake does not get injured.

Finding Prey

Rat snakes find their prey primarily by feel, sight, and scent. Apparently, they can see moving objects rather well (there is some question about whether snakes perceive stationary objects), and quickly orient on them.

Smell

In addition to sight, vibrations are noted and a rat snake's sense of smell is quite acute. Air- and ground-borne chemical cues are carried by the tongue to the sensory Jacobson's organs (in the roof of the mouth; see Glossary, page 123) where the odors are identified. Odors tell a snake what kind of prey (either alive or dead) is nearby and detect pheromones (odors from other snakes signifying their sex and willingness to breed). When a rat snake is hungry, the scent

A beautiful leopard rat snake eats a prekilled mouse.

of a prey animal elicits an immediate response, whether strike and hold or pursue and strike.

Overpowering Prey

Once the prey is grasped in the snake's jaws, it will be overpowered in one of two ways: by constriction (an effective method), or by throwing a loop of body over it and holding the prey animal as immobile as possible.

Constriction

Constriction does not result in broken bones or other such structural damage to the prey. Rather, with each exhalation of the prey animal, the constricting coils of the snake are tightened. Soon, inhalation is impossible and the prey suffocates. Some snake experts feel that this is a cruel death, but we can only state that Mother Nature is efficient, not kind, and it seems probable that most prey animals go into shock nearly immediately. Rat snakes are well capable of constricting two or more prey items at the same time; two separate constricting coils can be employed simultaneously. At times, prey may be pushed by a coil against the sides of a burrow or tree hollow. This is nearly as efficient a method of overpowering prey as actual constriction.

Positioning and Swallowing

Once the snake determines that the prey is ready to be eaten, positioning and swallowing begin. The snake may entirely release its hold on the prey, or maintain it. The tongue and the Jacobson's organ are used to find the prey's head (or more rarely, the feet) to begin the swallowing process.

Nearly everything about a snake, beginning with the jaw structure, is elastic. All tooth-bearing bones, both upper and lower, are capable of independent movement. Designed to retain a hold, the conical teeth are all recurved. To swallow its prey, the snake usually moves the upper and lower jawbones forward on one side. The same sequence now occurs with the opposite side. Once the prey is inside the throat, the neck and body muscles contract in sequence to push the prey into the snake's stomach. In essence, the snake "walks" its way around the prey animal. According to temperature and the metabolism of the snake, digestion may be slow or rapid. During this time, the snake is quieter than usual, often moving no further than is necessary to effectively thermoregulate.

What to Feed

Snakes do not feed entirely on live food, nor do some even prefer it. Some rat snakes in the wild find and eat long-dead rodents. Since we care about humane treatment of both predators and prey, we feed prekilled animals to all snakes that will accept them. We feed thawed, once frozen mice and rats. Though called rat snakes, the diets of none of these creatures is strictly limited to rats. For that matter, few of the species even limit their diets to the acceptance of endothermic (warm-blooded) prey.

The diets of many of the rat snakes change as they mature. In the wild, the juveniles of many seek lizards and frogs for their first few meals. With increasing size, there is more of a ten-dency for most rat snakes to become oppor-tunistic feeders and their diets are expanded to include nestling birds, eggs, and rodents.

Where a particular fondness for a specific food item is known, it is mentioned in the indi-vidual species account (see, for example, the comments made regarding the fondness of *O. rufodorsatus* for fish and frogs, page 110).

Size of Prey

We suggest that you offer prey that is sized to the snake: guppies (rarely), pinkies, or lizards to hatchlings or small snakes less than 14 inches long (35.5 cm); furred "jumpers" to snakes between 14 and 18 inches (35.5 cm–45.7 cm) long; small mice for young adult rat snakes 18 to 22 inches (45.7–55.8 cm) long; and adult mice or young rats to snakes larger than 22 inches (55.8 cm).

How Frequently to Feed

Feeding frequency depends on the snake and the time of year. During the summer months, rat snakes generally eat every week or every second week. During the winter months, those that do not actually hibernate will nonetheless

This is an albino yellow rat snake, **Pantherophis obsoletus quadrivittatus.**

greatly decrease their food intake to once every three weeks, or once a month, or even less frequently. Remember that snakes evolved along with their prey, and their appetites are closely attuned to the natural occurrences of their prey. Food is scarcer during the winter months.

Mice, rats and other rodents, anoles, and, sometimes, tree frogs are generally available at pet shops and specialty dealers across the United States, Europe, and in many areas of Asia. Often, "feed" rodents and lizards are considerably cheaper than "pet" rodents or lizards. Frozen rodents may be cheaper yet. Compare prices.

Because it is so easy to obtain domestic mice and rats, there is a tendency for hobbyists to try to induce even hatchling snakes to accept rodent fare. While this is acceptable, it is probably not natural, and although long lives are attained by our captive snakes, many herpetoculturists wonder how much better we would do (especially with "difficult" rat snake species) if we strived toward a more natural diet.

Prekilled food: A live rodent or bird can bite or peck a captive snake, causing additional stress to the snake or even irreversible damage.

We generally buy bulk lots of frozen mice from a reptile dealer and thaw the number needed in warm water, after which we blot them dry with paper towels, or at room temperature, or beneath a snake's basking lamp at feeding time.

Note: Because of internal hot spots, partial cooking, and deterioration of the body wall, don't use a microwave for thawing.

Using Wild Prey

We are often asked about the wisdom of feeding wild rodents—especially mice—to rat snakes. There are three points to consider here:

1. You must be absolutely certain that the wild rodent has ingested no rat or mouse poisons;

2. Be aware that wild rodents or their fleas can be carriers of serious diseases that are transmissible to humans;

3. Once they have eaten wild rodents, some rat snakes like them so much that they may be reluctant to accept domestic types again.

On the positive side, some rat snakes that are reluctant to feed on domestic rodents will eagerly accept wild species. We keep white-footed mice for just such contingencies.

Try Varying the Prey

Experiment with offering prey items of different species and colors. Some snakes will readily accept a newly born rat pup, but will steadfastly refuse a mouse of similar bulk. If they will accept neither rat nor mouse, try a hamster or a gerbil.

For Hatchling or Juvenile Rat Snakes

For hatchling or juvenile rat snakes, first try pinky mice, then pinky mice scented with tree frog or lizard odors, then tree frogs or lizards.

For Subadults and Adults

Subadult and adult rat snakes may accept the most conveniently available rodents (mice, rats, gerbils, hamsters). Then try baby chicks and/or button quail.

Reluctant Feeders

Try feeding a reluctant feeder during its major activity period. Some rat snakes are nocturnally active; some are diurnal. Check the species accounts for natural history notes. A secure snake will feed more readily than one that is stressed. Provide a hide box of some sort (see page 29) and place a prekilled food item in the doorway of the box. Make sure that your snake is kept at its optimum temperature. A rat snake that is stressed by being overly warm, or that is lethargic from temperatures that are too cool, cannot be expected to eat, nor will it usually do so. Regurgitation is also caused by unsuitable maintenance temperatures.

If your snake eats willingly, but prefers lizards over mice, scent the mouse with lizard's blood or even feces. We will often break the readily autotomized tail (which quickly regrows) off an anole, smear the droplet of serum that accompanies the break on the snout of a suitably sized mouse, and release the lizard. Rat snakes will frequently accept the scented mouse.

Keep the Meals Small

Small prey animals (whether alive or dead) are often more readily accepted by a rat snake than large ones. Two small prey items are more easily digested by the snake than one large food animal.

Small meals are also swallowed by snakes more easily and quickly. While this may make no difference to a well-adjusted specimen that feeds readily, if a nervous specimen or a poor feeder becomes stressed while eating, the snake is apt to lose the urge to feed or to disgorge a partially swallowed prey item.

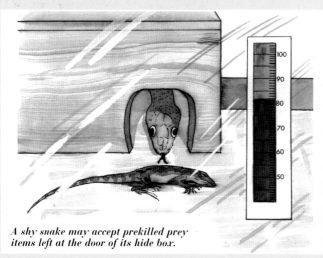

A shy snake may accept prekilled prey items left at the door of its hide box.

Force-Feeding as a Last Resort

Despite all of your efforts, there is the occasional rat snake that will not voluntarily accept an offered food item. In these cases, there is little recourse but to force-feed the specimen. Remember, the digestive system of a snake that has not fed in some time is probably compromised. Do not overfeed such a specimen; in fact, initially underfeed it. A compromised, basically nonfunctioning digestive system will be better able to digest a proportionately small meal than a large one. In force-feeding, you may use a "pinky pump"—a metal syringe with a large-diameter needle.

✔ Put pieces of pinkies inside the barrel of the pump.

✔ Lubricate the tip before inserting it down the throat, into the esophagus, of the snake. The unenhanced length of the tip of the pinky pump will allow sufficient insertion to feed a baby snake.

✔ If the pump is being used to feed a larger specimen, it may be necessary to affix a longer piece of smooth plastic tube to allow insertion for an additional distance.

✔ Use care—do not injure the gums, teeth, mouth lining, or glottis.

Another alternative is to actually place a small prekilled food animal far back into the snake's mouth and massage the food down the snake's throat. First, lubricate the mouse with water; some hobbyists prefer egg white. Next, insert the head of the rodent gently into the mouth of the snake. If done slowly and gently, the head of the mouse can be used to open the mouth of the snake. If at any time while you are doing this the snake begins to voluntarily swallow, slowly release your grip and allow the snake to eat. Often the snake will volunteer

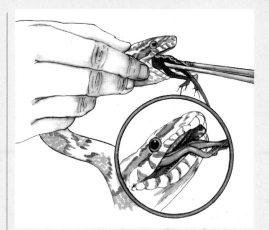

Place the food item far back in the snake's mouth, close the mouth, and wait to see if the snake will voluntarily swallow the item.

nothing and it will be necessary to slowly work the prey animal into and beyond the throat of the snake. Once pushed gently past the angle of the mouth, you will be able to work the rodent downward by gently massaging anterior to its position in the snake. If the snake shows little resistance, gently release it and see if it will work the prey into its stomach. If it begins to try to regurgitate, gently grasp the snake and massage the prey to a position a little closer to the snake's stomach.

Caution: In either case, force-feeding is traumatic for the snake and requires the utmost care on your part when you are doing it. Move slowly! This is important, for a startled snake is quite apt to fight the force-feeding or to regurgitate the meal once it is force-fed.

Do remember that the snake will have to be mostly immobilized during force-feeding. Even force-feeding may not always save a seriously debilitated snake, but it is worth making the effort.

BREEDING YOUR RAT SNAKES

Successful breeding a difficult species or selectively breeding for new colors or patterns is one of the greatest joys for any keeper. To start, you'll need a male and female rat snake, preferably of the same type and in good health.

Getting Started

The basics for breeding rat snakes are not complex, and a few general guidelines will give you enough information to begin. More detailed information is in the species accounts, beginning on page 54.

In an ideal situation, when placed together In the early spring, a male and a female snake will mate. In 30 days or so later, the female will lay her eggs, which will hatch in about 60 days. The babies will then have several weeks to feed and put on some weight before winter's cooler weather and shortened days naturally reduce their appetites.

That's the ideal scenario. In truth, you're going to have to provide the conditions that your rat

A hatching amelanistic corn snake greets the world.

snakes will find conducive for breeding—and you'll have to incubate the eggs so the young will emerge and be ready to feed.

Guidelines

The guidelines given here or in the species accounts for breeding your rat snakes are just that—guidelines.

If you or a friend are already successfully breeding rat snakes of a given species in a given area by using given methods, stick with your program. The guidelines described here worked for us in our facility in southwestern Florida. There we could successfully incubate many eggs at "room temperature" (always between 79 and 89°F [26–32°C], but most often between 82 and 86°F [28–30°C]). We had to work to reduce the relative humidity in the cages of arid climate species and to provide

Most rat snakes (like this Everglades race) can climb agilely.

suitably cool incubating temperatures for those species that did require full hibernation (or brumation—the terms are interchangeable) for reproductive cycling. Hobbyists and commercial breeders in the Pacific Northwest find it necessary to add heat to their caging systems for the majority of the year, and those in California or other areas of the Southwest may need to decrease or increase humidity and/or temperature. Herpetoculture is fraught with vagaries; what works well for one hobbyist may not be equally successful for another. But please share your methods with other hobbyists who have similar interests.

Resting Period

Many kinds of rat snakes, like other animals, need a wintertime resting period to help "time" or cycle their body for reproduction. How long a resting or hibernation period is needed depends on the kind of rat snake and where it's from. Rat snakes from a more northerly area or a higher altitude generally need several weeks of cooling to trigger the breeding response. Rat snakes from southern areas may need only a 30-day period of decreased temperature and lighting.

Find out where your snake originated and research the climatic conditions and microhabitats of that area to determine whether your snake needs cooling or hibernation/brumation.

Hatchlings and Hibernation

Hatchlings should not be brumated or hibernated during their first winter. Their appetites will decrease during the winter months, but they need year-round nourishment during their first year. Providing a resting or brumation period is not complex; in a nutshell, all you do is reduce cage temperature, lighting, and access to water and food.

After Posthibernation Shed

Following the posthibernation shed, put the sexes together. If courtship does not begin, mist the cage with water from a sprayer bottle. Point the bottle upward so the mist falls like a gentle spring rain on the snakes. This often inspires snakes to breed.

When breeding, snakes may stay coupled for hours, or they may breed once a day for a few days running. After mating, if you choose to do so, you can separate the sexes again.

Gestation and Egg Deposition

Gestating snakes need rather warm, secure areas in which to bask, and ultimately, to deposit their eggs (or in the case of the nonconformist O. rufodorsatus [see page 110], to give birth).

As with all other aspects associated with the keeping of rat snakes, the size of gestation and deposition/incubation sites must be tailored to the needs of your specimens. But generally speaking, the female will lay her eggs once she sheds for the second time after coming out of hibernation.

The Egg "Box"

An opaque plastic dish partially filled with barely moistened peat or sphagnum will often be accepted as a deposition site. The site becomes even more desirable to the snakes if it is covered, either by an opaque lid or by placing the tub in a darkened cardboard box. In both cases, be sure to cut an appropriately sized access hole. If the

═══ CHECKLIST ═══

Incubation Procedures/Techniques

✔ With the oviparous rat snakes, you need to provide correct temperatures during gestation and incubation. Incorrect incubation procedures can result in embryo deformity or death.

✔ Incubators can be either home-made or purchased. Chick-egg incubators from any feed store are big enough for several clutches of rat snakes and can be used year after year.

✔ Be certain you can regulate the temperature in the incubator you buy.

cage temperatures are inordinately cold, the corner of the cage bearing the deposition tub can be set on top of a heating cable or pad (set on Low) to increase warmth. Remember that heat from beneath will quickly dry the sphagnum or other medium and remoistening this will be necessary on a regular basis.

Female rat snakes will investigate their cages prior to laying their eggs—deposition—looking for the egg "box," the best spot in which to lay their eggs. Your female will probably spend some time resting in the egg deposition tub before she actually places the eggs there. Some snakes are a little slow to catch on—they'll spend days in the tub, moving only to lay their eggs in the water bowl. To avoid this, remove the water dish, replacing it for only an hour or so each evening.

Gravid female rat snakes may cease feeding a week, two, or even three, prior to egg deposi-

A leopard rat snake has shed its skin in the egg-deposition container.

tion. After egg deposition, offer food to the female. Small meals offered at frequent intervals seem best. Female rat snakes that retain or quickly regain their body weight following egg deposition will breed more frequently and successfully than underweight specimens or females that are slow to recover their weight.

The female will deposit her eggs several days following her next shed. One breeder in the Pacific Northwest has found his snakes will lay their eggs exactly ten days after that second shed.

Note: Once the eggs have been laid, take care not to wet them directly when remoistening the medium in the deposition tub.

The Babies

At the end of the incubation period—which may be as little as two weeks for some species, but is usually 60–70 days—the baby snakes will cut a slit in their egg with the egg tooth on the tip of their snout. The babies do not seem eager to leave the egg. They will cut a slit, look

out, and decide to stay inside the egg for a while longer, perhaps as long as a day and a half. Those that leave the egg can be removed to another terrarium and offered food, a sunning spot, and water. They should shed within a few days, and be ready for their first meal.

Although we prefer to keep the deposition boxes available throughout the year—the snakes use them as hide boxes during the nonreproductive season—some breeders place the boxes in the cage only during the breeding season. Remember that many snakes will multiple-clutch (lay more than one batch of eggs). Clean the box and replace the sphagnum (or other substrate) after the first deposition, but don't remove the deposition box early.

Fertile Eggs

By the end of the first week, those eggs that are not fertile will turn yellow, harden, and begin to collapse. Those that are fertile will remain white and turgid to the touch. Infertile eggs may mold, but this is seldom transferred to healthy eggs.

Temperature

The suggested incubation temperature is between 76 and 82°F (24–28°C), see species accounts, beginning on page 54, for details. Some slight variation of temperature may be desirable during incubation. Incubation humidity should be maintained at 80 to 95 percent. We keep an open container of water in the incubator.

Keep the incubator dark. Once laid, eggs can be gently moved but must not be turned. Frequent handling, rough handling, and excessively brilliant lighting are not good for the developing embryos.

Hatching

In nearly all cases, healthy full-term young will emerge from their eggs or egg membrane without incident. They will slit the egg with the help of an egg tooth on their upper lip, and will emerge within a day or two, peering out at intervals.

In rare cases, such as when the egg membrane dries too quickly due to improper humidity, the babies may need a little help escaping. Raising the relative humidity often seems to help the most. A short slit in the top of the egg or egg membrane may also help. Take care not to cut any blood vessels.

Caution: If you slit an egg prematurely, sometimes by only a few days, it can be fatal to the baby.

Sexing Your Rat Snake

"Probing," is the most reliable method of sexing subadult and adult rat snakes. When gently inserted into the hemipenial pocket of a male, a lubricated probe will slide smoothly back seven to twelve subcaudal scale lengths. If the snake is a female, the probe will insert only from two to four subcaudal scale lengths. If the probe is of incorrect diameter or is forced, injury to the snake may occur.

Hatchling rat snakes may be sexed by manually everting the hemipenes of males. This is done by placing the thumb a few scales posterior to the vent and rolling the thumb firmly, but very gently, forward. Females, of course, have no hemipenes to evert. Both sexing and manual eversion of the hemipenes is best learned from an experienced hobbyist.

Experience will also help you sex adult snakes just by comparing the shape and length of the tail. To accommodate the hemipenes, the tail of a male is broader at the base than that of a similarly sized female. Also, the tail of the male usually tapers less abruptly and is comparatively longer.

This Taiwan beauty snake may remain coiled in its egg for several hours before emerging.

HOW-TO: HIBERNATE YOUR

Reducing Ambient Temperatures

For those species that do not require a complete hibernation, reduce ambient temperatures in the room where you keep your snakes by switching from incandescent to fluorescent lights, turning off heating pads, opening room windows, or moving the cage to a cooler area. You don't need to freeze out your entire family; daytime temperatures of 78–83°F (26–28°C) and nighttime temperatures of 66–70°F (19–21°C) are usually adequately cool.

Using a Natural Photoperiod

If there is sufficient lighting from outside, the photoperiod will be no problem. If not, use a timer keyed to the sunrise/sunset times listed in your newspaper or from your local library.

Water and Feeding

Keep water available at all times and feed smaller meals at greater intervals.

At the end of the 30 days, restore your usual caging temperatures and lighting.

Hibernating Your Rat Snake

✔ Separate the sexes.

✔ Stop feeding two weeks prior to cooling. Do not feed during the cooling period.

✔ Reduce relative humidity by removing items from the cage that retain moisture, such as plants and the water dish. Or prepare a plastic container, such as a shoebox, to serve as the hibernation quarters.

✔ Clear a shelf in a cool, little-used closet in a basement or garage for the hibernation cages. Snakes need steady darkness and very cool temperatures for hibernation.

✔ Hibernation temperatures should be between 48 and 56°F (9.5–13°C). Hibernation duration is usually 8–10 weeks, but check your snakes' specific requirements

✔ Hibernating specimens should be roused for a drink every 15 days or so. Take the snake out of its box, place it on a shelf in front of you, and offer it water. After it drinks, place it back into its hibernation quarters. (Do not allow the snake to warm to room temperature.) If the snake does not drink, return it to its hibernation quarters and offer it water in a week.

✔ At the end of the hibernation period, simply replace your snake in its regular caging with water dish, hiding box, limbs, and plants, etc., in place.

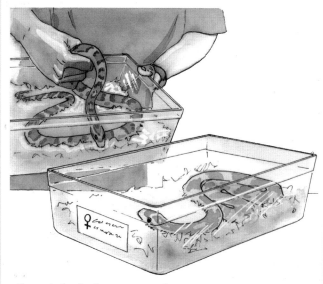

Covered plastic shoe or sweater boxes serve well as hibernating receptacles.

SNAKE

After Hibernation

Before feeding your snake following hibernation, allow it to remain warm for several days once it is removed from brumation (the proper term when referring to reptiles and amphibians). It is also best to feed a newly warmed snake proportionately small meals before giving it normal size prey. For example, if your rat snake generally eats adult mice or half-grown rats, offer it a pudgy pinky mouse or a rat pup for the first one or two meals.

Allow your snake time to digest and stool between meals. Once you have determined that your rat snake's digestive system is working well, you may increase the size of the prey.

Once your snake is removed from hibernation, it is *very* important that it has fresh drinking water available at all times. This cannot be stressed enough. An inadequately hydrated snake may have difficulty in digesting even a small meal and this can, and usually will, result in regurgitation of the prey.

Fluctuating cage temperatures can also cause regurgitation at this time. Make sure that a basking spot ("hot spot") providing a temperature of 82–90°F (27–32°C) is available around the clock. Because it will allow a natural photoperiod, an under-terrarium heater is better than a lightbulb. As long as the hot spot is available, ambient terrarium temperatures can be allowed to fluctuate.

Should your rat snake regurgitate, do not offer it food again right away. Wait one week before attempting to feed it again and then offer an even smaller meal.

Other Changes

Whether your rat snake is cooled or actually hibernated, physiological changes occur to it

Hibernating snakes should be provided with cool temperatures and darkness.

during dormancy. During hibernation, rat snakes cycle for a post-emergence shedding of the skin and for breeding.

Skin shedding will usually occur within two or three weeks after emerging from hibernation. In preparation for shedding, your rat snake will become dull and the eyes will turn blue and milky. At this time, because the snake is incapable of seeing well and may be more susceptible to predation and injury, it will often remain in hiding. While preparing to shed, snakes often refuse food. This is a normal reaction and should not be cause for concern. At this time the outer skin can tear very easily, causing injury to the developing new skin. Great care should be used if it becomes necessary to handle your rat snake while it is preparing to shed.

Although some reproductive pheromones may be present prior to skin-shedding, they are the strongest and most compelling after ecdysis. Pheromone trails left by females in the wild enable males to trail, encounter, and breed with them.

The identification of, and husbandry techniques for, species of rat snakes available in the hobby in 2006 are presented here. Specialized needs, however, are discussed in the individual accounts section.

Rat Snake Taxonomy

The rat snake names you may be familiar with may no longer exist. In recent years, increased reliance on genetic studies has divided the long-standing rat snake generic name of *Elaphe* into several smaller genera. An additional proposal has realigned the American rat snakes.

Although we continue to include the Western genus *Senticolis* in this book, recent DNA tests suggest that this genus may actually be more closely allied to gopher snakes than to rat snakes.

Those changes that seem to have been well accepted by the herpetological community have been incorporated into this revised book.

Here's what those changes mean

✔ All North American rat snakes formerly in the genus *Elaphe* are now in the genus *Pantherophis*.

This is a juvenile western fox snake,
Pantherophis vulpinus.

✔ Based on genetic differences, a new species of corn snake from Louisiana, *Pantherophis slowinskii*, dubbed Slowinski's corn snake or the Kisatchie corn snake, has been identified.

✔ It has been suggested that the Great Plains rat snake is now a full species rather than a subspecies of the corn snake.

✔ A genetic realignment of the American rat snakes once known as *Elaphe obsoleta* has been proposed. Rather than numerous sub-species of a single species, these snakes are now contained in four full species. Divided on an east to west basis, the Atlantic seaboard species is *Pantherophis alleghaniensis*. Next west is *Pantherophis spiloides*. The species of the central states is *Pantherophis obsoleta*, and the southwesterlymost representative is *Pantherophis bairdi*.

We have elected to retain the traditional species-subspecies nomenclature herein, but agree that the generic name should become *Pantherophis*.

The New Nomenclature
If not listed, the names have not been affected by recent changes.

Old Name	New Name	Common Name
Elaphe bairdi	Pantherophis bairdi	Baird's rat snake
Elaphe cantoris	Orthriophis cantoris	Eastern trinket snake
Elaphe conspiccilata	Euprepiophis conspicillatus	Japanese red rat snake
Elaphe erythrura	Coelognathus erythrurus	Asian reddish rat snake
Elaphe flavirufa	Pseudelaphe flavirufa	Mexican night snake
Elaphe flavolineata	Coelognathus flavolineatus	Yellow-striped rat snake
Elaphe guttata	Pantherophis guttatus ssp.	Corn snakes and Great Plains rat snakes
Elaphe helenae	Ceolognathus helenae	Trinket snake
Elaphe hodgsonii	Orthriophis hodgsonii	Himalayan trinket snake
Elaphe hohenackeri	Zamenis hohennackeri	Transcaucasian rat snake
Elaphe janseni	Gonyosoma janseni	Sulawesi black-tailed rat snake
Elaphe longissima lineata	Zamenis lineatus	Lined Aesculapian snake
Elaphe longissima	Zamenis longissima	Aesculapian snake
Elaphe mandarina	Euprepiophis mandarinus	Mandarin rat snake
Elaphe moellendorffi	Orthriophis moellendorffi	Moellendorff's rat snake
Elaphe obsoleta	Pantherophis obsoletus	Black, yellow, gray, and Everglades rat snakes
Elaphe perlacea	Euprepiophis perlaceus	Pearly rat snake
Elaphe persica	Zamenis persicus	Persian rat snake
Elaphe porphyracea	Oreophis porphyraceus	Bamboo rat snake
Elaphe quatuorlineata sauromates	Elaphe sauromates	Bulgarian rat snake
Elaphe radiata	Coelognathus radiatus	Radiated rat snake
Elaphe rufodorsata	Oocatochus rufodorsatus	Red-backed rat snake
Elaphe scalaris	Rhinechis scalaris	Ladder snake
Elaphe schrenckii	Elaphe anomala anomala	Amur rat snake
Elaphe situla	Zamenis situla	Leopard rat snake
Elaphe subradiata	Coelognathus subradiatus	Indonesian rat snake
Elaphe taeniura	Orthriophis taeniurus	Beauty snake
Elaphe vulpina	Pantherophis vulpinus	Fox snake

Snow corn snakes are among the coveted designer colors.

✔ The genus *Pseudelaphe* has been erected for the Neotropical night snakes.

✔ The generic name of *Elaphe* is restricted to a few European and Eurasian rat snakes.

✔ In addition to the long-standing generic name of *Elaphe*, the generic names of *Coelognathus, Euprepiophis, Oocatochus, Oreophis, Orthriophis, Rhinechis,* and *Zamenis* have been erected for various Old World rat snakes.

Meet the Corn Snake

What's in a name? Today, the names used by hobbyists for some snakes and those used by researchers are not always identical. Over time

and with varying outlooks on taxonomy, both scientific and common names have changed. Because this book is intended primarily for hobbyists, we have attempted throughout the text, and especially in the species accounts, to cross-reference the old names with the new. For example, until rather recently, whether it came from New Jersey, Florida, or Louisiana, a corn snake was just that, a corn snake, and the Great Plains rat snake was a subspecies of the corn snake. Some geneticists, using DNA analysis, have divided the corn snake into two full species and consider the Great Plains rat snake a full species as well. We suspect it will take a while before hobbyists accept and begin to use these new names.

The Kisatchie corn snake from western Louisiana is considered a distinct species by some researchers.

Where Corns Are Found

Not only is the corn snake, *Pantherophis g. guttatus*, found over an immense area in the southeastern United States, it is common across that range. When you add to this the incredible beauty and color plasticity of the corn snake it is small wonder that this wonderful reptile has become the most popular pet snake.

Throughout its range the corn snake may be found in a variety of habitats; a snake that is able to successfully utilize a variety of habitats is called a habitat generalist. It ranges south-ward from southeastern New Jersey to the southernmost tip of the Florida Keys, and from those states west to central Kentucky and east-ern Louisiana. (It has been suggested by some researchers that the Louisiana corn snakes are a separate species to which the scientific name of *P. slowinskii* has been assigned, but that desig-nation is not widely accepted.)

The corn snake intergrades with the westerly Great Plains rat snake in northwestern Louisiana, southcentral Arkansas, and extreme eastern Texas. Occasionally, natural corn snake-black rat snake complex hybrids are found.

Genetics 101

At the outset of the captive-breeding craze, line-breeding corn snakes for desired color or pattern traits was a simple matter. Most of the breeders available were wild-collected speci-mens that carried few, if any, aberrant charac-teristics. If you wanted to breed for darker corn snakes, you could simply linebreed the dark corn snakes to dark corn snakes, and breed their darkest young to each other. Pretty soon you'd end up with *really dark* corn snakes. Or, if you wanted to breed for a recessive trait, simple Mendelian genetic principles applied. Today, though the same genetic principles apply, it is a different matter entirely. After 25 years of color and pattern manipulation, corn snakes now carry such an extensive hodgepodge of color genes that it is entirely possible to breed to like-appearing specimens and have three or more entirely different color morphs appear in the progeny from that breeding.

To begin to understand the complexities involved, you'll need to learn a little bit about genetics. Simply put, a snake is considered heterozygous for a trait if it carries both a dominant and a recessive gene or allele for the same trait. If the snake has both a dominant and a recessive allele, the dominant gene will mask the recessive. If the snake has two recessive alleles, the recessive coloration or trait will appear. We'll use albinism (amelanism) as an example:

A corn snake that is heterozygous for albinism appears normal, because the gene for normal coloration is dominant (or masks) the gene for albinism. Breed two heterozygous snakes together, and the offspring will receive one allele for coloration from each parent. A Punnett chart, named for the man who developed it, demonstrates the process; each snake is heterozygous for albinism, but that albino gene (a) is masked by the dominant gene for normal coloration (A):

	A	a
A	AA	Aa
a	Aa	aa

Each parent contributes either a dominant (A) or recessive (a) gene for coloration, and how these genes pair up in the young determines the color. One-quarter of the young will be homozygous for the normal coloration (AA), and appear normal in coloration. One-half will be heterozygous—Aa; the dominant gene is listed first—and will also appear normal in coloration. The remaining quarter of the young will be homozygous for albinism (aa), or albinos.

Of those normal-appearing snakes, two-thirds will bear the gene for albinism (Aa), while the remaining third will bear the gene for normal coloration (AA). You can tell which snakes bear which genes only by breeding the normal-appearing snakes together and seeing what their young look like. Their young are called the F1 generation, or first filial generation. If the parents have one dominant and one recessive gene for albinism, the F1 young will have the same mix as their parents' chart, above. If you breed a heterozygous and a homozygous together, their young will look like this:

	A	A
A	AA	AA
a	Aa	Aa

All the young will appear normal, but half of them will bear the gene for albinism. If you breed these young together, if both adults bear the recessive gene for albinism, albino young will result.

If you breed two albinos together, you'll be breeding what is called double recessives—each parent can contribute only the recessive gene for albinism. Those offspring will all be albinos, because no dominant genes are in their gene pool.

As you can tell, keeping accurate records of the genetics of each snake you produce is critical to predict what will be the result of any future breeding. It may take several generations before you acquire enough albino—or any other recessive trait—stock to breed together to produce nothing but albinos.

When breeding for albinism began, we thought there was just one type of albinism—a snake lacking pigment, with pink eyes. That type of albinism is a simple dominant/recessive allele. Now we know that there are different types of albinism; there are complete albinos, partial albinos, albinism that affects only specific regions of the snake's body (like a piebald corn snake), and genetic-defect albinos. This last type of albino possesses nonfunctional melanophores, the cells that form dark pigment. One type, Type B amelanistic, lacks tyrosinase, the enzyme that permits the formation of melanin. The second type, Type A amelanistic, has a tyrosinase inhibitor that prohibits the passage of tyrosine, a melanin precursor, into the melanophores.

Lavender corns lack all traces of red.

Colors of Corns

The brightest: The most brightly colored corn snakes seem to occur in the central Atlantic states, and those on both the northern and southern peripheries of the range tend to be smaller than the corn snakes from the interior areas. The ground color may vary from orangeish (the "normal" phase) to gray (southern Florida) to brownish (a rare phase in southwestern Florida); however, west of the Mississippi, the corn snakes rather uniformly assume a darker, drabber hue, and are called the Great Plains rat snake; the old, outdated name is Emory's rat snake, *Elaphe guttata emoryi.*

"Normal": What Is "Normal"?

The term refers to the coloration of the usual wild-caught specimen, and this varies somewhat geographically. The basic corn snake is a dull orange snake with often narrowly outlined black-edged red dorsal and lateral blotches. The venter is prominently checkered with black and white. Hatchlings are less colorful than adults. Most corn snakes available today are captive bred and hatched. It is probable that more than 40 morphs are now available (it's a little hard to keep track!).

Corn Snake Species

Okeetee Corn Snake

Over the years, the term "Okeetee phase" has come to mean the prettiest of the pretty corn snakes.

Coloration: This phase, named for a hunt club in southeastern South Carolina, is typified by bright scarlet saddles, broadly edged with jet black, set against a ground color of vibrant red-

This is the pretty intermountain (Utah and Colorado) phase of the Great Plains rat snake, **Pantherophis guttatus emoryi.**

orange. The belly is also orange, although usually paler than the sides or back, and checkered with jet black.

Habitat: Although this phase is often said to be restricted to the low country of southeastern South Carolina and immediately adjacent Georgia, Okeetee phase corn snakes may be encountered both to the north and the south of that area. Okeetee now connotes brilliance of color and contrast of pattern rather than geographic origin.

The Miami Phase Corn

This snake, with its maroon on pearl gray theme, is a familiar sight in much of the southern third of the Florida peninsula. This amazingly resilient snake persists in some areas of downtown Miami. All it needs there is some cover, water, and a food supply.

The "Rosy Rat Snake"

This snake is found to the south of the Florida mainland, in the Florida Keys. This is a much sought-after, somewhat smaller, morph of the corn snake.

Coloration: These variably colored corn snakes occur in three color phases: olive, silver, and rosy. When compared with mainland corn snakes, all of the Keys morphs have reduced black pigment. Once designated as *Elaphe guttata rosacea*, the rosy—also called the Keys corn—is now thought to be merely a variant of

Corn snakes from east Texas are usually brown and gray.

the red rat snake, or *P. guttatus*. Many of the corn snakes of the Florida Keys as well as many of those from Pinellas and Hillsborough counties show very reduced amounts of black in their patterns.

The Kisatchie Corn

This is a dully colored phase of the corn snake that occurs in western Louisiana and eastern Texas.

Coloration: The ground color is a light olive brown and the saddles are dark olive brown.

This snake was long thought to be an intergrade between the corn snake and the Great Plains rat snake, but DNA data has shown it to be merely a dark corn snake. It has been recently described as *Pantherophis slowinskii*.

Designer Corn Snakes

Axanthic: An axanthic corn snake lacks functioning xanthophores, the cells that produce yellow and red pigment. These snakes are also called anerythrystic (without red). A corn

Corn snakes from the lower Florida Keys may be orange (pictured), silver, or olive.

snake without red or yellow is black and gray. Born a somewhat pallid combination of black and gray, their colors intensify and they accumulate considerable yellow near the sides of the neck. This pigment is thought to result from dietary carotinoids accumulated within the xanthophores.

Amelanistic: Amelanistic or albino Okeetee corn snakes are occasionally advertised as "reverse Okeetee phase." On these, the normally wide black markings that surround the dorsal and lateral blotches are replaced by equally wide borders of white and the black of the belly is lacking. The ground color is orange and the blotches are coral or deep red. If you like albinos, this is a pretty mutation.

Blood-red: This interesting phase of the corn snake, despite its color, is not an albino, although an albino strain has been developed. The blood-red originated from selectively breeding some of the prettier and redder corn snakes found in northcentral Florida. The adults of this morph are nearly a uniform deep red dorsally and laterally, and a somewhat paler red,

TIP

Conservation

Practice conservation—find, watch, and photograph—but leave the animal in its habitat for others to also see and enjoy—and to assure future wild generations.

often patterned with diffuse blotches of white, ventrally. The black that normally outlines the dorsal saddles is entirely lacking. Hatchlings are less intensely colored. They have a light ground color and rather well-defined dorsal saddles as well as some lateral blotches and a gray head. Sadly, the hatchlings of the blood-red corn snake may prove delicate and can be among the most difficult to induce to feed. Even once started, not all thrive. If you are considering a purchase of this morph, be sure to insist on feeding specimens.

Amelanistic (or white albino): Adults of this beautiful snake have, when in the "normal" phase, a pale pinkish body and strawberry to coral dorsal and lateral blotches. Since it is the black pigment that is absent in this form of albinism, the snakes have a particularly contrasting pattern. White albinos are among the most commonly produced of the aberrant corn snakes, and were the first of the throng of truly aberrant colors to be readily available to hobbyists. The juveniles have an almost white ground color and strongly contrasting coral-red blotches.

Sunglow: This is an enhanced red albino corn snake. It is typified by a lack of all white fleck and saddle outlines. When adult, this coveted color phase is an interesting study of weakly defined coral or deep-orange blotches on a paler orange ground color. The hatchlings are much paler than the adults.

Candy cane: This color morph is typified by precisely outlined, deep red to red-orange blotches that contrast sharply against the almost white ground color. The overall appearance is quite pretty.

Snow: Once considered the ultimate mutation, snow corns are now very common in herpetoculture. They originated when both amelanistic and anerythristic mutations were selectively bred together. Snow corns have a pearl white ground color and the somewhat metallic-looking, pearl white, pale yellow, to pale lime dorsal blotches are precise but faded and pale. With increasing age a wash of yellow, orange, pink, or green may develop on the ground color. If present, this suffusion of color will be brightest anteriolaterally.

Ghost: This mutation is variable, but often looks somewhat like a rather brightly marked snow corn or a pale anerythristic corn. These snakes are defined by breeders as hypomelanistic (reduced black) anerythristics. They are of an almost translucent pink at hatching and turn pinkish lavender with growth.

Blizzard: The blizzard corn is a further refinement of the snow corn. The pattern of the blizzard corn is all but invisible. In essence the blizzard corn snake is a white snake with bright ruby eyes.

Hypomelanistic (or "hypo"): In appearance this morph looks rather like a pale, strongly patterned, blood-red corn snake. It is typified by a reduction (but not complete absence) of melanin and deep red blotches on a ground color of orange-red. The dorsal and lateral sad-

This is a young adult Great Plains rat snake from the Big Bend region of Texas.

dles are partially outlined with a very thin edging of black.

Christmas: The mutant known as the Christmas corn snake was developed by Bill Brant of Gainesville, Florida. Like the hatchlings of most corn snakes, those of the Christmas corn are rather dull, giving little indication of the pale greens and crimsons that will develop with age. This mutation is the result of selectively breeding certain insular South Carolina corn snakes.

Butter: Although some of the terms used for describing newly developed corn snake phases can be confusing, you need only to see a butter corn sake to realize the name is entirely accurate. This snake was developed by Rich and Connie Zuchowski (Serpenco) of Tallahassee, Florida. When we saw the snakes, we were pleasantly surprised. Among the hundreds of yearling corns of all phases being sized by the Zuchowskis, the butter corns were pretty and immediately identifiable. The adults, which we saw in normally blotched and motley phases, were truly beautiful. The ground color is a buttery yellow, and the blotches, which may have a light center, are a rich yellow-orange. This color phase has also been referred to as an "amelanistic caramel" and a "snow-caramel" corn snake.

Pepper (also referred to as Pewter): This phase has been derived from breeding a charcoal (type B tyrosinase negative anerythristic corn snake) with the blood-red phase. The colors are muted, and in some cases the pattern is only weakly defined.

Lavender: As with all corn snakes, both the ground and pattern colors of this phase can vary. Normally, the ground color is of some shade of purplish gray (lavender?) and the

This pretty olive phase corn snake is from the lower Florida Keys.

darker purplish brown pattern, which may be outlined with even darker pigment, is well defined. This color phase is also known variously as "mocha," "chocolate," or "cocoa."

Amber: By breeding the hypomelanistic trait into the caramel phase, corn snakes with very pale, light-centered, caramel saddles have been developed. These snakes have a pale gray ground color. They are marketed as "amber" corn snakes.

Caramel: This is another interesting corn snake morph developed by Serpenco. It was derived from breeding a wild-collected corn snake that had enhanced yellow in its pattern with a snow corn. This now rather stabilized color morph has a pale gray ground color and yellowish red saddles with only a hint of dark outlining.

Pattern Mutations

Motley pattern: The term "motley" refers to a pattern anomaly that is quite variable. The pattern may assume the form of partial striping and/or "H" (ladder)-like blotch connections. The saddles may be as wide as the light pigment between them or they may virtually dominate the snake. Whether wide or narrow, large or small, the blotches are best defined middorsally and meld—at times almost imperceptibly—with the yellowish lateral coloration. If present at all, the lateral blotches and ventral pattern are greatly reduced. Albinos (amelanistics) and melanistic (anerythristic) specimens also may bear this unusual pattern.

Striped pattern: Striping is a pattern anomaly that is now readily available. Like the motley trait, the recessive striped trait reduces belly

The Gulf Hammock rat snake is an intergrade between the gray and the yellow rat snakes.

patterns. However, unlike the irregular dorsal patterns of motley corns, the four-striped pattern of the striped corn snakes is rather constant. These snakes bear two heavy dorsolateral stripes and two less well-defined lateral stripes. Striping has been developed in Okeetee and normal corn snakes as well as in snow, blood-red, anerythristic, amelanistic, and other mutants.

Aztec pattern: This phase of the corn snake combines a dorsal pattern of rather normal-appearing, but irregularly edged blotches in a zigzag pattern. The overall effect is of a pretty corn snake with an exceptionally busy pattern.

Milk snake pattern: The normal examples of the milk snake phase corn snake combine the gray ground color of the Miami phase corn with saddles that are broader than normal. Many combine high contrast with attractive colors, but there are some that appear suffused with olive or pale brown. Continuing manipulation, incorporating amelanistic and motley patterned corn snakes into the mixture, has produced some colors and patterns that are even more interesting.

Creamsicle: This is the name given the amelanistic (albino) intergrade between the corn snake and its Western race, the Great Plains rat snake, *P. g. emoryi*. While the "normal" intergrade produces a snake that typically is brighter than the Great Plains but duller than the corn snake, when the mutation for amelanism is factored in, the offspring produced have a beautiful yellow-white ground color and peach to pale orange blotches. The color intensity of these magnificent intergrades intensifies with advancing age.

Candy cane: This is another color phase of an amelanistic corn snake. Occasionally these are interbred with a Kisatchie corn snake or

This is a dark phase yellow rat snake from the Florida Keys.

Great Plains rat snake in an effort to allow the removal of the melanin to lighten the dark background color even more. The unedged dorsal blotches of this morph are cherry red and contrast strongly with the stark white ground color.

The Great Plains Rat Snake

The Great Plains rat snake is the most westerly and the least colorful of the corn snake clan. There are two rather weakly differentiated subspecies. The subspecies *Pantherophis g. emoryi* is the northernmost of the two races, and *P. g. meahllomorum* the southernmost. As mentioned earlier, some taxonomists now consider the Great Plains rat snake a full species. In one or the other of its subspecies, the Great Plains rat snake ranges from southwestern Illinois and southeastern Nebraska southward to Louisiana and northeastern Mexico. Over much

of its range *P. g. emoryi* is an abundant and interesting serpent. For the most part it is a pleasing combination of gray on gray. It attains an adult size of 4½ feet (135 cm) in length and the record length is only 5¼ feet (153 cm).

Subspecies: *P. g. emoryi* has 45 or more dorsal blotches and usually 18 tail blotches. This subspecies is found to the north and west of south Texas. *P. g. meahllmorum* has 44 or fewer dorsal blotches, 17 or fewer tail blotches, and ranges southward from south Texas to northeastern Mexico. The disjunct population of Great Plains rat snakes in eastern Utah and adjacent Colorado was once considered a subspecies *(P. g. intermontanus)* but it is now recognized as *E. g. emoryi*.

Color morphs: Because Great Plains rat snakes are so dull when compared to the more easterly corn snake, not many hobbyists seek them out. Of the commonly seen "designer

The black rat snake, Pantherophis o. obsoletus, *has an immense range across the eastern United States.*

corns," the Great Plains rat snake has contributed its genes to the "creamsicle corn." Albino Great Plains rat snakes have been found, but most of those now seen in captivity have albino corn snake genes somewhere in their background.

Amelanistic: As in the corn snake, examples of the amelanistic Great Plains rat snake lack melanin. Typically, this morph has a white ground color and small pink dorsal saddles that are not outlined with a contrasting color. Hatchlings and juveniles are more richly colored than the adults.

Chocolate: Don Soderberg has been stabilizing this very dark color morph of the Great Plains rat snake. The strain has been developed by selectively breeding a dark individual found in Kansas. The ground color is so dark brown that the dark saddles are not easily seen.

Hibernation: Since most Great Plains rat snakes originate from cooler areas than corn snakes, a period of actual hibernation may be required to cycle them for breeding. A reduction in winter temperature (to 45–52°F; 8–11°C) and photoperiod for 70 to 90 days is recommended.

Finding a Corn Snake in the Wild

Over their range, corn snake populations may vary from rare—often on the peripheries of the range—to common, or actually abundant. They and all other herpetofauna are protected by some states, but may be legally collected in others.

To find a corn snake, on a warm, sunny day in spring, summer, or fall, go to where the snakes are—the edges of old agricultural fields (corn and soybean are favored, hence the name—"corn snakes")—woodland edges, especially those where litter is strewn about, or even urban areas where some cover remains. Walk slowly along the field and woodland edges, turn debris; especially roofing tins or other such cover in the early spring, but be careful! Venomous snakes also seek such cover.

Corn snakes can also be found by road hunting. When the weather is warm, slowly drive along old country roads in the early evening. Corn snakes often cross these. Remember that finding a corn snake doesn't mean you have to collect it. It might be a better idea to leave that corn snake in the field; it's certainly easy enough to buy a captive-bred specimen in color morph of your choice.

Hobbyists have readily accepted the licorice rat snake (a strain of white-sided black rats).

Keeping and Breeding the Corn Snake

Feeding: As adults, captive corn snakes thrive on rodent prey. Most hatchlings and virtually all juveniles do likewise. In the wild, hatchling corn snakes are as apt to feed on amphibians and small lizards as on rodents.

An occasional hatchling, even from multiple-generation captives, may insist on lizards or tree frogs at the beginning. These holdouts can usually be switched to pinky mice within a few meals by scenting the pinky with the preferred prey species. Scent the pinky less with each feeding, then desist entirely. We use the term "usually" because a small percentage of captive-bred corn snake babies never feed, and die as a result.

Size and behavior: The moderate size (commonly to 4.5 feet [1.3 m], rarely to 6 feet [1.8 m], the official record) and inordinate tractability of corn snakes make them an ideal species for even novice keepers. The "designer colors" now available, and the possibility (even probability) that a new color or pattern will appear in any clutch of hatchlings, tends to hold the interest of even long-time hobbyists.

Eggs: Corns may produce from six to about twenty eggs. More than one clutch may be laid annually. Smaller and younger females tend to lay smaller clutches than older and larger females.

Hibernation (brumation): Hibernation is not necessary to breed most corn snakes. If you choose to brumate your corn snake, a temperature between 45°F and 52°F (7–11°C) for a period of 90 days is satisfactory. Some breeders retain their snakes in total darkness during hibernation; others allow a natural, unenhanced photoperiod.

Bubblegum rat snakes are albino intergrades between the black rat snake and the yellow rat snake.

Winter breeding: Corn snakes will also cycle for breeding if they are merely cooled (not hibernated) during the winter. To accomplish this, allow winter (December, January, and February) temperatures to drop by a few degrees during the day and a few more at night, and allow an entirely natural photoperiod. The breeders continue to eat, but meal size and feeding frequency are reduced. For a resting period, water should always be available. With such a regimen, corn snakes cycle reproductively and breed readily.

The Black Rat Snake and Its Subspecies

Blacks, Yellows, Grays, and Texas

These are the American rat snakes, being essentially restricted to the eastern United States. A small population of the black rat snake is found in Canada on the eastern end of Lake Ontario.

For beginners: From the standpoint of hardiness, the several members of this group are ideal starter snakes. They do well either with or without a period of winter dormancy, although those from northern areas seem to need winter dormancy for reproduction. Most feed readily year-round if kept warm. The captive-breeding industry supplies most of those in the pet market, which in turn lessens the number of specimens taken from the wild. Captive breeding has resulted in albino (amelanistic) and other designer morphs.

Catch your own: If you live in or visit the eastern United States, you can usually catch your own black rat snake. They may be found beneath litter in open fields, along rocky ledges, or sunning on sloping tree trunks. The only

A lack of scales (except for the belly plates) is one of the most unusual aberrancies. This is a scaleless yellow rat snake.

drawback to catching your own is that the adults will often bite if they feel threatened. And although they are nonvenomous, a bite from one of these large and impressive snakes is more than a little disconcerting to most folks. Black rat snakes tame with gentle handling.

Subspecies

Five subspecies of *Pantherophis obsoletus* are currently recognized: the black rat snake, *P. o. obsoleta*; the yellow rat snake, *P. o. quadrivittata*; the Everglades rat snake, *P. o. rossalleni*; the gray rat snake, *P. o. spiloides*; and the Texas rat snake, *P. o. lindheimeri*.

Additionally, at least four easily distinguishable intergrades, three of which were once themselves considered subspecies, are known: the Gulf Hammock variant, *P. o. spiloides* x *P. o. quadrivittata* (once designated as *Elaphe o. williamsi*), the Keys variant (a dark orange-brown, striped, and blotched creature formerly called *Elaphe o. deckerti*), and the dusky, dark-striped narrow blotched morph from the Outer Banks of North Carolina that was once called *Elaphe o. parallela*. The common name of this drab beast was the Outer Banks rat snake. The black rat-yellow rat intergrade from the Carolinas and elsewhere, where the ranges of the two races abut, is often referred to as the greenish rat snake.

Tree-dwellers: *Pantherophis obsoletus* complex snakes are largely arboreal but can be found in roadside dumps or amid other human debris. In certain areas of Florida, yellow and gray rat snakes, their intergrades, and corn snakes can be found by shining a strong flashlight beam upward into roadside or canalside trees after dark. In the past, yellows, corns, and

Everglades rat snakes were abundant in pump-houses that controlled crop irrigation, despite the all-pervasive smell of diesel fumes.

The Black Rat Snake

The black rat snake, *P. o. obsoletus*, is the largest of the several *obsoletus* subspecies. With a record size of 101 inches (2.56 m), it is one of the largest snakes in America.

The specific name *obsoletus* means dim, probably referring to the snake's subdued coloration.

Range: The black snake is the northeastern-most *obsoletus* member. It ranges from the southern tip of Ontario, southern Massachusetts, and southeastern Minnesota, southward to northern Louisiana and central Georgia. It is largely absent from the coastal plain of the Carolinas where it is replaced by the smaller but more brightly colored yellow rat snake.

Coloration: Even though normally a dark color and hence less visually appealing than a brighter snake, the black rat snake is a favorite of many reptile enthusiasts, beginner or expert. It is common, impressive, and hardy. At least two genetically distinct albino forms are available, and to make things even more complex, a fair number of intergrades between albino black rat snakes and other races are now available to hobbyists under names that may, or may not, reflect their lineage.

The normal coloration of the black rat snake varies considerably over its wide range. The darkest (blackest) individuals seem to come from the Northeast and the mountains of the Southeast.

Specimens that we have found in the southern Blue Ridge Mountains have been every bit as dark as specimens we have found in the Berkshires of Massachusetts. On the other hand, black rat snakes from the western part of the range are often more brown than black. The largest individuals tend to be the darkest. Under bright light, the dark blotches of babyhood can still be seen on most. It is the light ground color of the babies that becomes suffused with melanin, finally obscuring the dorsal blotching.

The interstitial skin is often lighter, being white or reddish, and the throat is light (often white). The light gular coloration may extend for a variable distance onto the venter.

The two albino morphs: These differ dramatically from each other. One is a mostly white snake with reddish saddles and red eyes. The other is much redder, often being lavender to pale red with brilliant strawberry dorsal saddles. Interestingly, different genetic factors determine the color abnormalities of these two snakes. Thus, when the two are bred together,

Unusual color aberrancies are occasionally seen in the wild. This very dark yellow rat snake was found in central Florida.

to the surprise of most breeders, the resulting offspring are of the normal, pigmented coloration. There are other morphs beyond the two albinos.

The white-sided variant: This well-established variant has white sides and a black back. It is also referred to as the licorice or licorice stick rat snake.

The leucistic variant: This is a stark white, unpatterned black rat snake with blue eyes. Examples are readily found in the pet trade. It is a favorite of hobbyists.

A "brindle" variant: This variant, having variably reduced melanin (hypomelanism), is now also available. In color, this form may vary from a light tannish pink with reddish blotches (brightest and best defined anteriorly), to a rather uniformly patterned gray-brown on dirty tan. These snakes may not be particularly pretty, but they are very different!

This abnormally pale yellow rat snake was found in Glades County, Florida.

The albino bubblegum rat snake: This is a very pretty snake "mutt" with a combined lineage of Everglades, yellow, and black rat snakes. With growth, the babies develop pink blotches on an almost white ground color, with variable highlights of yellow or pale orange. The ads for these claim that "no two are identical."

The Yellow Rat Snake

The subspecific name of the yellow rat snake, *P. o. quadrivittata*, refers to the four rather prominent lines borne by adult specimens. The common name refers, of course, to the ground color of the adults. Like all members of this species group—except the Everglades rat snakes, which are light in color—juvenile yellow rat snakes are quite dark, having a gray ground color and nearly black saddles.

Range and color: The range of yellow rat snakes extends southward along the coastal plain from just south of North Carolina's Albemarle Peninsula to the central Florida Keys. The most intensely colored specimens occur on the extreme south of peninsular Florida to the region of Big Pine Key.

Over most of its range, the yellow rat snake retains its own subspecific integrity, meaning it does not seem to interbreed with other members of the genus. This, the second largest of the *obsoleta* rat snakes, is known to occasionally exceed 7 feet (2.1 cm) in length.

The ground color varies from straw yellow to rather bright yellow. The stripes can be broad or narrow and dark, or rather poorly defined. Those on the northern and western peripheries of their range tend to be a duller yellow than specimens from the coast and the southern portions.

The adults in some populations retain vestiges of the juvenile saddles and in some areas

This color morph of the yellow rat snake is found on the southernmost peninsula of Florida and the northern Keys. It was once referred to as Deckert's rat snake.

(Cape Coral, Florida, for one) adults retain well-defined saddles and lack stripes.

Albino yellow rat snakes have been found and are now being bred. These specimens retain the saddles; the stripes are poorly defined.

Intergrades: The greenish rat snake is a naturally occurring intergrade between the yellow and the black rat snake. It is common where the ranges of the two subspecies abut in areas of Georgia, extreme southern South Carolina, and on northward to southeastern Tennessee. Often a dingy olive color when adult, the four stripes are usually prominent.

The Gulf Hammock variant of northwestern peninsular Florida is also a naturally occurring intergrade between the gray rat and the yellow rat snakes. A grayish ground color, this variant retains the juvenile saddles and develops the usual yellow rat four stripes. Of the naturally occurring rat snake variants, the Keys or Deckert's rat snake is the most attractive. Like the Gulf Hammock animal, the Keys variant retains the juvenile saddles and develops stripes. However, its ground color is yellow-orange, deep orange, or brownish orange, and the tongue is black. The saddles can be prominent or vague and brownish to maroon in color. The prettiest animals are those with the deep orange ground color and maroon saddles. Apparently, this snake has never been common. Today, a Keys variant rat snake is considered much harder to find than the rosy rat variant of the corn snake (see page 66).

Everglades rat snake: *Pantherophis o. rossalleni* is the most colorful member of this species group. The subspecific name is a

The Everglades rat snake, **Pantherophis obsoletus rossalleni,** *has the most orange of the group.*

patronym for Ross Allen, an herpetologist/showman of Florida in the 1940s and 1950s.

These big orange snakes with obscure striping were distinctly recognizable residents of inland Florida south of Lake Okeechobee prior to the 1980s. As the Everglades drained, the yellow rat snake followed the drying land southward. It has interbred so extensively with the Everglades race that the latter has been almost extirpated.

Everglades rat snakes can exceed 6 feet (1.8 m) in total length. At that size they are definitely impressive. The body, head, chin, and eyes are an often rich orange. The tongue is entirely red. Black tongue pigment would indicate a "visiting" yellow rat snake in the fairly recent lineage.

The stripes of the Everglades rat snake do not usually contrast strongly with the ground color.

Captive-breeding successes: Does this mean that Everglades rat snakes are gone entirely? Fortunately, no. Through selective breeding, herpetoculturists have kept this race alive and well, perhaps even enhanced. Not only are Everglades rat snakes produced each year, but a hypomelanistic phase has been developed. With the reduction of the melanin, the body color of these adults is a resplendent red-orange. This snake looks more like what we think an albino ought to look like than the albinos themselves do.

Other morphs: Another project involving Everglades snakes has produced a recessive blotchless phase. Not even the hatchlings have the normal dorsal blotches. Other striped subspecies have been worked in here and the phase is now available in normally pigmented and amelanistic morphs.

The Gray Rat Snake

Very little linebreeding or other genetic enhancement has been done by breeders with the gray rat snake, *P. o. spiloides*. The gray rat snake is the deep South's lighter-colored version of the North's black rat snake.

Color: There are two color phases of the gray rat snake—the rather dark, gray on gray "normal phase," and the lighter, prettier gray on grayish white "white oak phase." The dark dorsal saddles, which this subspecies retains throughout its life and to which the subspecific name of *spiloides*, spotted, pertains, of the normal phase are often bordered with an even darker, narrow edging. Those of the white oak phase are often narrowly edged with a very light gray. The saddles may be completely dark or light-centered. Gray rats retain the blotches of babyhood.

Tree-dwellers: Gray rats are opportunistically arboreal. Although they may be seen on the

The "white oak" phase of the gray rat snake, **Pantherophis obsoletus spiloides,** *(above) has a less busy pattern than the normal phase.*

As pictured here, some Texas rat snakes, **Pantherophis obsoletus lindheimeri,** *are quite colorful. Others may lack the orange hue.*

ground, they are as often seen high in trees and in the rafters of deserted buildings.

Size: The biggest recorded gray rat was 84.25 inches (2.13 m).

Range: Gray rat snakes may be encountered from coastal Panhandle Florida to western Mississippi. From there they range northward to northern Alabama and the somewhat warmer Mississippi River valley to extreme western Kentucky, southeastern Illinois, and immediately adjacent Indiana.

The Texas Rat Snake

If you are enthralled by belligerence in a snake, let us introduce you to the Texas (or Lindheimer's) rat snake, *P. o. lindhiemeri*, named for herpetologist Fred Lindheimer. There may be no other harmless snake in America quite so ready to bite.

Coloration: The Texas rat snake is another of the *obsoletus* subspecies that retains the blotches throughout its life. In coloration, most Texas rats are lighter than a black rat and darker than a gray rat. The ground color can vary from straw yellow to orange, but more usually tan or light brown. The dorsal blotches are rather elongate, fairly narrow, and medium to deep brown, either with or without light centers. The contrast between the dark dorsal blotches and the lighter ground color is not very great.

The lateral interstitial skin can vary from yellow to orange. The interstitial color may spill over onto the leading edges of some lateral scales, but since the trailing edge of the preceding scales overlaps, the little brilliance may not be seen unless the snake is distended with food or tightly coiled.

Baird's rat snakes from Mexico tend to be more richly colored than their Texas counterparts.

Other obsoletus morphs: Actually, few hobbyists work with normal, wild-caught Texas rat snakes, although many keep and breed two of the most common mutants—an albino (actually amelanistic rather than a true albino), and a leucistic (see Glossary, page 123). Of the two, the albino is the less pretty, being white (almost translucent when hatched) with pink saddles. The colors intensify somewhat with increasing age. The dorsal saddles of older adults are usually pale strawberry. The eyes of the amelanistic are pink.

The leucistic morph is a beautiful creature. It is a solid, unpatterned white and has gray-blue eyes.

Reproduction: Both the size and age of the snake determines sexual maturity. All the *obsoletus* are oviparous and, if fed heavily, most can attain sexual maturity in their second summer. Even slow growers usually are sexually mature by their third year of life.

Females of 3 feet (0.9 m) in length can successfully breed and produce fair-size clutches of eggs. A 32-inch-long (81-cm) female yellow rat snake, which was actually slender for her size, produced five viable eggs. Small and young specimens have fewer and smaller eggs than older, larger adults. The clutch of an old, healthy female—anywhere from four years of age and up—often numbers 25 or more eggs. The eggs are easily incubated; suggested temperature: 82–86°F (28–30°C) and hatch in 60 days. The hatchling snakes are robust and easily reared. Hatchlings can exceed a foot (30 cm) in length, and some 16 inches (40 cm) long have been reported.

Many Baird's rat snakes appear to have an opalescent overlay of color.

The Baird's Rat Snake

(*P. bairdi* ssp.)

Baird's rat snake is a denizen of the arid Chihuahuan desertlands in western Texas and northern Mexico. It is often found along roads.

Appearance: Although the colors of the moderately sized Baird's rat snake are muted, it is a pretty, easily handled, and very hardy rat snake. Dorsally, adult Baird's rat snakes may vary from a dusty pearl gray through a powdery orange-brown to a rather warm burnt orange. Adult males are usually suffused with more and brighter orange than females.

Adults have four dark to orangish stripes of variable intensity and contrast. The pair of dorsolateral stripes are usually the better defined.

The brighter specimens, especially those with orange striping, seem to come from the southernmost part of the range: the Mexican states of Nuevo Leon and Tamaulipas. The interstitial skin and often the anterior edge of each scale may be a rather bright orange. The entire snake may have orangish overtones, brighter anteriorly. The venter is usually an unpatterned yellow to orange.

Hatchlings and juveniles are grayish with a busy pattern of many thin dorsal saddles. Lateral blotches are also numerous and rather well defined. A curved dark bar crosses the snout immediately anterior to the eyes and a dark postocular stripe runs from eye to mouth. With growth, both markings pale and eventually disappear completely. The head of an adult Baird's rat snake is entirely without markings.

Western fox snakes are not uncommon but are seclusive.

Baird's rat snake (the name honors Spencer Fullerton Baird, a nineteenth-century vertebrate zoologist) was originally considered a subspecies of the very wide-ranging *P. obsoletus*. It is a moderately heavy-bodied snake with a maximum size of just over 5 feet (1.5 m). Females are generally longer than the males; the males are usually more orange than the females. Two color morphs, the Mexican and Texas, are now being bred by hobbyists. The Mexican differs from the Texas specimens by a gray head and a ground color suffused with orange. Now that some market interest is being shown, these once rather expensive snakes will become more common and perhaps less pricey.

Reproduction: Although these snakes seem to reproduce best if hibernated, pairs have produced viable eggs with little more than a slight winter cooling and a reduction of photoperiod. Hatchlings are about a foot (30 cm) in length.

Clutches number from four to ten eggs. Incubation nears 90 days at 82–86°F (28–29°C). The hatchlings almost always feed readily on newly born mice. Large, healthy females often produce two clutches annually.

The Two Fox Snakes

Until recently, the two fox snakes, the eastern and the western, were considered subspecies of the same species. Today they are considered two full species: the western fox snake, *Pantherophis vulpina*, and the eastern fox snake, *P. gloydi*. This separation seems a reasonable approach, for at no point are the ranges of the two contiguous, nor do the two naturally intergrade.

The fox snakes have probably derived both their common name and their scientific name of *vulpina* from the scent of the musk produced by the anal glands. To some the odor is reminiscent of the red fox; in any case, it is a musky odor best avoided by not frightening the snakes.

Reluctant Feeders

Although they are quite pretty, neither of the fox snakes is popular as a captive. Like many northern latitude snake species, fox snakes taken from the wild, especially in the fall as they near hibernation, can be problematic feeders. This reluctance to feed is natural for snakes in the wild, as they would soon be entering hibernacula (see Glossary, page 122). In captivity, subjected to warm temperatures and continued activity, these snakes can lose a fair amount of body weight before they are again ready—both physiologically and psychologically—to feed.

Coloration: Despite being from different areas, the two fox snakes are difficult to distinguish if the origin of the specimen is not known. The ground color of both tends toward straw yellow, and the dorsal and lateral blotches—an average of 41 between nape and tail on *P. vulpina* and 34 on *P. gloydi*—are dark. The head of the adults of both species can be orange to coppery red, although *P. gloydi* is more apt to be the brighter. Unfortunately, the reddish head often leads to the fox snakes being mistaken for a copperhead and summarily killed. The fact that these snakes nervously vibrate their tails in the leaves when approached leads to an alternate erroneous identification. Hearing the "whirr," these big constrictors are also often mistakenly identified as rattlesnakes.

The juveniles of both tend to have a paler ground color than the adults and also have the blotches edged in black or darker brown. A head pattern is usually discernible, the most prominent markings being a transverse bar between the eyes and a dark postocular stripe that angles downward to the angle of the jaw. The head markings fade to obscurity with advancing age.

Ranges: The western fox snake is found over a fairly extensive range. It occurs in agricultural areas, marshes, and open woodlands from the western portion of Michigan's Upper Peninsula southward along the western and southern shores of Lake Michigan to Illinois and northwestern Indiana, and from there westward in complex fingers of range to southwestern Minnesota, southeastern South Dakota, and eastern Nebraska. It barely enters Missouri in the extreme Northwest and again in the extreme Northeast and a tiny portion of the eastern central prairieland.

The eastern fox snake is far more circumscribed in range. This species can be encountered in suitable (but ever-dwindling) patches of habitat along the shores of Lake Huron as well as the western and northern shores of Lake Erie. Less of a habitat generalist than the western fox snake, the eastern species seeks marshlands and open woodland edges associated with marshes. Because of this restricted habitat, the eastern fox snake is considered an imperiled species by most researchers.

Captive behavior: Most of the few fox snakes that enter the pet trade are wild-collected specimens of the western species. Newly collected fox snakes may strike and bite savagely, but quiet down with gentle handling.

Try to acquire your specimens in the spring, when they are more apt to feed. Once acclimated and feeding, fox snakes can make interesting, long-lived captives. Adult size is about 4 feet (1.2 m) in length. Occasional specimens of either species may exceed 5 feet (1.5 m).

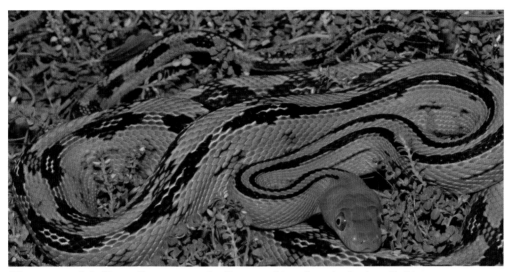

This pretty adult Trans-Pecos rat snake, **Bogertophis subocularis,** *is coiled in roadside grasses.*

If hibernated, fox snakes can be bred. Egg clutches are large, often exceeding 20 eggs. An incubation temperature of 80 to 86°F (27–30°C) is suggested. The foot-long (30-cm) hatchlings usually feed readily and grow quickly.

The Trans-Pecos and Baja Rat Snakes

These two American rat snakes are the sole members of the genus *Bogertophis*. Both are slender snakes with big heads and "bug-eyes." Both were long considered members of the genus *Elaphe*. Their current generic name commemorates the contributions to herpetology by the late Charles M. Bogert. The two species contained in this genus are *B. subocularis*, the coveted Trans-Pecos rat snake—two subspecies, both referred to as "subocs" by hobbyists. The second species is the poorly known Baja rat snake, *B. rosaliae*, which is often called the Santa Rosalia rat snake.

Scales: Both of these snakes share a characteristic unknown in other North American rat snakes: They bear an extra row of scales that separate the eye from the upper lip scales. Called suboculars, it is from these scales that the Trans-Pecos rat snake derives its scientific name.

Range: As one might expect after observing the proportionately large eyes, these snakes are primarily nocturnal. They may be encountered as they cross roadways or forage among canyonside boulders, from a few minutes after nightfall until the early hours of the next morning. Rather than being rare, it is their secretive nocturnal habits that make these desert dwellers seem so.

These are warmth-loving arid climate snakes that fare poorly as captives in areas of high

The blonde morph of a Trans-Pecos rat snake is an uncommon and coveted snake.

humidity, such as on our southeastern coastal plain or in fogbelt regions. However, when both air conditioning and winter heating reduce the relative humidity, these snakes do well.

The Trans-Pecos Rat Snake

Range: *Bogertophis s. subocularis* ranges southward from central New Mexico and western Texas to the Mexican states of Durango and Nuevo Leon. This is a beautiful snake that occurs in three distinct morphs. There is also a poorly known central Mexican subspecies.

✔ The "normal" phase of the Trans-Pecos rat snake occurs over most of the range of the species. The ground color of this morph is straw to olive yellow. The neck is marked with a pair of (usually) distinct black dorsolateral stripes that fades and becomes H-shaped blotches on the body. The arms of each H are formed by a darkening of the dorsolateral stripes. The cross-bar of each H may be as dark as the arms and considerably paler or lacking entirely. (The latter seems especially apt to occur on captive-bred and hatched specimens.) Poorly defined lateral blotches are often evident.

✔ A "blonde" morph occasionally occurs in the lower Pecos River drainage, especially near Ter-lingua, Texas. The ground color of this phase is much yellower than normal and the dorsolateral striping, even on the neck, is either muted or absent. Rather than Hs, the body markings are in the form of light-centered, irregular saddles. Lateral blotches may, or may not, be present.

✔ The third morph is less well known. The markings are like those of the normal phase but, rather than being yellow, the ground color is pale to steel gray. These gray subocs seem restricted in distribution to the Franklin Mountains, a range near El Paso, Texas.

Selective breeding has produced a silver Trans-Pecos rat snake.

Several albino subocs have now been found. A pretty gray phase has been developed and is now being captive bred. This phase is often referred to as the silver morph. It is quite different in appearance and sells for much higher prices than the normal subocs.

Mexican subspecies: Because the snake is protected in Mexico, no examples of the subspecies, *B. s. amplinotus*, are known in herpetoculture. In this race the neck striping is dark and of uniform width and the dark blotches are variable and seldom in the form of Hs. The dark blotches are wider than the light interspaces and the dark lateral spots are very evident; thus, the snake appears to be dark with light barring. This is in direct contrast to the nominate form that always appears to be a light snake with dark blotches. *B. s. amplinotus* seems restricted in distribution to the southernmost periphery of the range of the species.

Diet: Although these snakes reach a fairly large size and bulk, captives prefer small prey items. In our experience, adults readily accepted baby mice or newborn rats, but might refuse larger prey. Although these snakes can constrict, they often simply immobilize their live prey with a coil. Hatchlings may prefer small lizards, especially the sideblotched lizard, *Uta stansburiana*, or anoles, *Anolis* sp.

Size: When adult, the Trans-Pecos rat snake may be 5½ feet (1.65 m) in length.

Reproduction: The Trans-Pecos rat snake tends to be a late breeder, with the female going through two (or, rarely, three) posthibernation sheds before being ready to breed. Breeding can occur as late as June, with the eggs being deposited in August or September. From three to seven eggs are laid. The eggs should be incubated from 82 to 86°F (28–30°C).

Availability: In its normal phase the Trans-Pecos rat snake is both readily available and relatively inexpensive. Blonde phase specimens are in more limited supply and generally cost at least twice as much as the normals. The silver morph is in short supply and is, at present, very expensive.

The Baja Rat Snake
(*Bogertophis rosaliae*)

Range: The range of this poorly understood snake extends northward from the southernmost tip of the Baja Peninsula to Imperial County, California. Once thought to be rare, it is now known that it is the isolation of the range and habitat of this species that makes it seem uncommon. Since Mexican wildlife laws prohibit the collecting and exportation of this species to the United States except under specific permits, it will probably never be common in herpetoculture.

Coloration: This interesting snake is almost unicolored when adult and hardly any better patterned when small. Hatchlings are so light in color that they appear translucent. The adult coloration may vary by specimen from olive tan or olive green to reddish brown. The babies are paler and have thin, poorly defined white (or at least lighter) dorsal crossbands.

Size: This slender snake attains an adult size of 5 feet (153 cm).

Diet: Captives seem to prefer small prey items such as baby mice and will usually accept newborn rats. Although capable of constricting, this snake often simply immobilizes live prey with a single loop and swallows it. Although a few hatchlings will feed on newly born mice, most prefer suitably sized lizards. The favorite lizard type seem to be side-blotched lizards, *Uta stansburiana.*

Reproduction: The Baja California rat snake is another late-breeding snake, with the posthibernation female shedding two or three times before breeding. Breeding may not occur until June. Eggs are deposited in August or September.

Availability: Specialty breeders occasionally offer hatchlings of *B. rosaliae* to the public. The cost of these remains several hundred dollars per snake. Despite this high price, specimens are usually snapped up quickly. The facts that there are few breeding-size Baja rat snakes in U.S. collections, that they are not the easiest of the rat snakes to breed, and that those that do breed produce small clutches will keep the price of the species high in the foreseeable future.

The Green Rat Snake and Relatives

The green rat snake, *Senticolis triaspis intermedia,* ranges southward from Arizona well into Central America. The recent finding of several green rat snakes in southeastern Arizona suggests that this snake is more secretive within its restricted southwestern range than rare. South of the border this snake takes on a russet tinge and may retain the juvenile blotches until well into adulthood.

Description: The head is distinctive in shape, being elongate, somewhat flattened, and rather broad temporally. At the tip, the snout is rather square. The most northerly green rat snakes truly are green, at least when they are adults. The juveniles are rather prominently marked

The Baja rat snake, Bogertophis rosaliae, can vary from olive tan to reddish tan.

In the United States the green rat snake, Senticolis triaspis intermedia, *is found only in southeastern Arizona.*

with black-edged brown dorsal saddles and lateral blotches against a yellowish ground color. Both juveniles and adults have an unmarked yellow belly.

Second subspecies: The reddish brown "green" rat snake from Central America is of the subspecies *mutabilis*. Like the race *intermedia*, as adulthood is reached, the blotched pattern of the southern race become obscured and large adults are almost (or entirely) unicolored.

Third subspecies: Unlike the two races already mentioned, *Senticolis triaspis triaspis* from the Yucatan Peninsula, Belize, and adjacent Guatemala, retains the saddled juvenile pattern throughout its life. This, the nominate subspecies, *S. t. triaspis*, is found both in thorn scrub forest and on more open agricultural lands. Both juveniles and adults have dark-edged brown dorsal and lateral blotches against a lighter ground color.

Captive care: Whether you call it the green rat snake, the Yucatan rat snake, or some other contrived common name, most hobbyists consider *Senticolis triaspis* a difficult captive. This seems especially so of specimens from the northern portion of the range. Like many subtropical snakes, especially those that feed opportunistically on lizards, frogs, and endothermic prey, wild-collected *S. triaspis* usually harbor a great load of endoparasites. Even after these have been purged, this rat snake can prove problematic.

Although a riparian species, captives fare poorly if subjected to long periods of high relative humidity. Northernmost specimens seem particularly prone to respiratory ailments and digestion problems. The northernmost specimens also seem particularly distressed by both warm and cold temperature extremes. They prefer, and fare best, when temperatures are main-

Adult **Senticolis triaspis mutabilis** *are often russet.*

tained in the mid-70s°F (21–24°C). Specimens from the southern regions seem less sensitive.

Diet: This is one of the rat snake species that prefers small-sized meals. Pinky mice will usually be eaten and digested; mice of larger sizes may be refused, or, if eaten, later regurgitated. Males, which seem to be the smaller sex, are particularly reluctant to accept anything but small rodents. Wild-caught snakes show a definite preference for wild, rather than domestic, mouse species. Hatchlings of all subspecies seem to prefer lizards over rodents.

Needs in captivity: Despite all of these problems, green rat snakes and their more southerly relatives are eagerly sought by advanced breeders. Prices are high for specimens, whether acclimated or freshly collected from the wild. These finicky snakes demand fairly elaborate facilities with controlled temperature and humidity. Adequate cover, such as hide boxes and other visual barriers, will help these nervous snakes feel at home. Although primarily

terrestrial, if their cage is large and limbs are provided, these rat snakes may climb agilely and frequently.

Breeding: A few specialist breeder hobbyists have succeeded in keeping and breeding green rat snakes. Most of these people live in areas very close to the natural habitat of the snakes, such as Arizona, New Mexico, and southern California. A period of winter dormancy seems as mandatory for successful long-term husbandry as for reproductive cycling. Brumation can be a critical period for these snakes. One breeder reported that when a "hot spot" was provided near the hibernaculum, cooled *Senticolis* will often preferentially keep their heads and anterior bodies warmed while positioning their posterior body in the cooled hibernaculum. However, other individuals who work with green rat snakes merely cool them the same as they do other montane species and report no unusual problems when the snakes are warmed the next spring.

Baby Senticolis have well-defined saddles.

A clutch consists of from 2 to 10 eggs. At an incubation temperature of 80 to 83°F (26–28°C) the eggs will hatch in 65 to 85 days. Hatchlings are 12 to 14 inches (30–35 cm) in total length. Hatchlings will usually accept newly born mice.

A Latin American Corn Snake Look-alike

Pseudelaphe flavirufa is known as the Mexican night snake. Since the species' range extends south of Mexico, the name is not entirely accurate. *Pseudelaphe flavirufa* is a beautiful and relatively hardy snake that is now bred by many hobbyists. Both normal and anerythristic morphs are available. The ground color of the normal morph is gray. The dorsal and lateral markings are outlined in black and vary from strawberry to maroon in coloration. The dorsal markings may consist of discrete blotches or may be connected for all or part of the length of the snake. The anerythristic morph is patterned similarly, but lacks the red and yellow hues.

The Mexican night snake darkens noticeably with age and very old adults are much less attractive than younger specimens. The several subspecies are poorly differentiated (see chart, page 85).

The eyes of this very nocturnal snake are proportionately large and have stark white irises.

Size: These snakes reputedly attain a length of more than 5 feet (1.5 m) in length, but 26 to 40 inches (66–102 cm) is more common.

Reproduction: Although these snakes come from areas that are subtropical in climate, they often hail from cool, rather dry areas of this very indefinite climatic designation, and others from warm and quite humid areas. Since we have not

Subspecies	dorsal blotches mostly connected (zigzag)	dorsal blotches discrete	lateral blotches well defined	lateral blotches absent	preocular divided X undivided Y
flavirufa	X		X		Y
pardalina	X		X		X; 31 scale rows
polysticha	X		X		X; more than 32 scale rows
phaescens		X	X		
matudai		X		X	

The ranges of the various subspecies are:
flavirufa: the east coast of Mexico, from the state of Tamaulipas southward to Campeche
pardalina: mainland Guatemala, Honduras, and Nicaragua
polysticha: Caribbean Islands of Honduras
phaescens: Mexico's Yucatan Peninsula
matudai: poorly known; southeastern Mexico

bred this species, we can offer only suggestions for its herpetoculture. We would subject them to a period of winter cooling (but not true hibernation) for a period of 60 to 90 days.

Our largest specimen, a 40-inch (101.6-cm) female, was gravid when received. She eventually deposited five eggs that were incubated at room temperature (79–85°F [26–29°C]). The incubation period, although not specifically recorded, was in the vicinity of 60 days. The hatchlings had a paler ground color than the female.

Diet: *P. flavirufa* seems to prefer meals both small in amount and in size.

Captive care: Although the Mexican night snake is not a particularly active captive, it should be provided with a secure hiding area.

A portrait of a Mexican night snake.

European rat snakes are not common in America, yet are routinely kept in Europe. Imports by dealers are usually hatchlings and are quite expensive.

European and Eurasian Rat Snakes

American hobbyists generally consider European rat snakes to be delicate, which perhaps can be attributed to the American mind-set for keeping reptiles in the simplest possible way. Maybe the European hobbyists' tendency to construct elaborate terrarium environments pays off for these snakes.

Of course, another factor may figure in—shipping. At best, shipping is stressful for snakes. Most Europeans acquire their European rat snakes by hand, carrying them from origin to terrarium. In America, specimens must be shipped, which takes from two to four days of temperature variations, inspections, air pressure

The Celebes black-tailed rat snake, Gonyosoma janseni, may be gray, tan, or black.

variations, and bouncing around. If the rat snake is then dropped into an unadorned plastic shoebox, it's small wonder that these snakes seem delicate.

Eurasian Distribution

Of the four species of rat snakes that occur in Europe, only the ladder snake, *Rhinechis scalaris*, is restricted to that continent. The other three are found well into western Asia; therefore, they are actually of Eurasian distribution. Only one European rat snake species, the leopard rat snake, *Zamenis situla*, is brightly colored as an adult.

A final note before moving on: All European rat snakes seem to need lengthy periods (±80 days) of full hibernation (at 48–54°F [9–12°C]) to cycle reproductively. Do not expect to breed them without this period of complete dormancy. Sadly, many of them seem prone to respiratory problems during hibernation. Use care and inspect your animals often.

TIP

European Hobbyists

European hobbyists covet their rat snakes and few breed as readily as the American corn and yellow rats. Most (if not all) European countries also now largely prohibit collecting reptiles and amphibians from the wild. Since virtually all specimens that are available are captive bred and hatched, eager and sophisticated European hobbyists provide a ready market.

If you hope to work with the European species and are willing to pay for them, going for a more elaborate caging set up may pay off.

At a temperature of 79–82°F (26–28°C), the incubation duration for the eggs of all European rat snakes ranges from about 58 to 75 days. Although some hobbyists prefer the lower temperature, we have had the best success with 81–82°F (27–28°C).

The Ladder Snake
(*Rhinechis scalaris*)

Markings: A good alternate name for the young adults of this moderately sized rat snake would be "two-lined rat snake." The dark transverse bars of the busily patterned young become obscured with increasing age, leaving only a pair of dorsolateral lines. A dark postorbital blotch angles downward to or beneath the rear of the jaw in younger specimens. This becomes obscure with increasing age. The markings of some old adults can be almost totally obscured.

Disposition: The ladder snake is of variable disposition. Wild-collected adults can be savage, but many captive-bred animals are rather tractable.

Coloration: The ground color of adults may vary between brown, brownish olive to yellow-olive dorsally and laterally. The venter is somewhat brighter, often yellowish or off white in color, but may be suffused with dark pigment. The ground color of juveniles is brighter. The ladder of the juveniles and adult lines are darker brown than the ground color. This is an interesting, but not brightly colored, snake.

Size: Although adults of the ladder snake occasionally attain a length of more than 5 feet (1.5 m), most individuals range from 4 to 4.5 feet (1.2–1.37 m) in length.

Not discussed in the text, Coelognathus erythrurus, the Asian reddish rat snake, is a slender species from the Philippines.

The ladder snake, Rhinechis scalaris, *is a rather small Asian species.*

Range: The range of *R. scalaris* is restricted to the Iberian Peninsula, southern coastal areas of adjacent France, and some outlying islands. It prefers dry, rather open habitats, and is typically encountered in terrestrial situations in agricultural areas, open, rocky woodlands, hedgerows, and near rock walls, all favored basking sites.

Habits: Wild specimens bite readily. Captive ladder snakes are most active in the late afternoon and at dusk.

Diet: Although the adults strongly prefer endothermic prey of moderate size (mice, small rats, birds, etc.), the diet of the juveniles can also include lizards, frogs, insects, and what baby endotherms they happen across.

Captive breeding: This species has been bred in Europe and America. Typically, clutches number between four and nine rather large eggs.

The Four-Lined Rat Snake
(*Elaphe q. quatuorlineata*)

Size: Although usually only 4.5 to 6 feet (1.06–1.8 m) long, adults may attain 8 feet (2.4 m) in length. This is the largest of the European rat snakes. This big rat snake is relatively calm in captivity, but will bite when it feels threatened or eager to feed.

Coloration: This intriguing snake undergoes great color and pattern changes as it matures. The hatchlings and juveniles are prominently spotted with dark dorsal and lateral blotches on a pale gray or tan background. The top of the head is spotted and a large, posteriorly divided nape blotch is evident. A dark postorbital bar is present.

With growth, the spots, including those on the surface of the head and the nape, become obscure and the four dark lines for which the

Elaphe sauromates is now called the Bulgarian rat snake.

species has been named become increasingly prominent. The dark postorbital bar is usually retained. The ground color darkens to deep tan, brownish olive, or light brown. The ground color is darkest vertebrally. The top of the head is brown and the lips are light. Some examples, especially *E. q. muenteri* from the Aegean Islands, retain the juvenile blotching and develop striping as well.

Range: The four-lined rat snake ranges from the Aegean Islands to Italy, Greece, and the southern Balkans.

Breeding: Up to 18 eggs may be laid per clutch.

Diet: *Elaphe q. quatuorlineata* is one of the hardier and more voracious of the European rat snakes. Although hatchlings may show a preference for lizards, most will readily accept pinky

mice. Larger-sized snakes will accept correspondingly larger mice or small rats.

The Bulgarian Rat Snake
(*Elaphe sauromates*)

Until recently, this snake was considered a subspecies of the four-lined rat snake. This rat snake retains the juvenile blotching throughout its lifetime.

Range: It ranges from northeastern Greece and southeastern Bulgaria through the Danube region to the Caucasus, Asia Minor, and Iran.

Size: The Bulgarian rat snake seldom exceeds 4.5 feet (1.37 m) in total length.

Breeding: A clutch may contain from 2 to 7 eggs.

The Aesculapian Rat Snake
(*Zamenis longissima*)

The often gentle *Z. longissima* was considered sacred by the ancient Greeks and has since been associated with Aesculapias, the Greek god of medicine. A caricature of this species is depicted on the medical caduceus.

Coloration: Adult Aesculapian snakes are olive tan to olive green and may bear the vaguest vestiges of dorsolateral striping and/or light flecking. A dark postocular bar is very visible on juvenile specimens and, although faded, may be retained into adulthood.

Except for their smooth scales, hatchlings and juveniles of the Aesculapian rat snake look remarkably like the young of *Natrix natrix*, the Eurasian grass snake—complete to the alternating dorsal and lateral checkers and the yellow to off white temporal blotches. There are three poorly defined subspecies of Aesculapian snake.

Range: Only *Z. l. longissima* has been available to American hobbyists. The nominate form ranges from the eastern Iberian Peninsula eastward through southern Europe, to extreme northwestern Iran. *Zamenis l. persica*, a dark-bellied race, occurs in northern Iran.

Habitat: Like other European rat snakes, *Z. longissima* is a primarily terrestrial snake associated with dry, sandy, sunny habitats that provide cover in the form of vines or other open vegetation. Old rock walls, hedgerows, ruins, and dry, open woodlands are also prime habitat.

Diet: This snake often prefers several small, rather than one or two large, mice. Hatchlings and juveniles will eagerly accept lizards. Most will, however, quickly convert to meals of pinky mice.

Breeding: Cycling *Zamenis longissima* for breeding will require a 60 to 120 day period of hibernation at 48–54°F (9–12°C). Watch for any signs of respiratory problems during this period. After emerging from hibernation, breeding usually occurs following the postemergence skin-shedding. Between 2 and 12 eggs are contained in a clutch. When incubated at 80–82°F (26–28°C), eggs will hatch in 50 to 65 days. Hatchlings are from 10 to 12 inches (25–30 cm) in length.

The Leopard Snake
(*Zamenis situla*)

We come now to the crown jewel of European rat snakes. As a matter of fact, the leopard rat snake—a corn snake lookalike—is one of the world's most beautifully colored snakes. Baby specimens that are not used to being handled may bite repeatedly, but with gentle handling, leopard snakes soon tame.

Coloration: Leopard rat snakes may be variably marked. The black-edged strawberry dorsal markings may be in the form of two rows of

A portrait of the leopard rat snake.

Zamenis situla is referred to as the leopard rat snake.

The Aesculapian rat snake is now known scientifically as Zamenis **longissima.**

discrete spots, a single row of vertebral saddles, or stripes. Normally the ground color is a pale gray. Anerythristic morphs have been found. These have a dark gray ground color, darker dorsal markings, and lack most if not all red coloration. The head pattern is rather complex. A dark, posteriorly curving bar extends across the top of the head immediately anterior to the eyes. The internasals are usually tipped anteriorly with some black. A diagonal black temporal stripe is present on both sides and a black, or black-edged red marking extends anteriorly from the partially divided nape blotch on to the frontal plate. The venter is predominantly black. Leopard rat snakes are proportionately slender.

Size: The leopard rat snake is the smallest of the European rat snakes. An average size for adults is between 26 and 30 inches (66–75.6 cm). An occasional exceptional specimen may near 40 inches (101.6 cm) in length.

Habitat: Like other European rat snakes, *Z. situla* is associated with hot, dry, often sandy, rocky, or sparsely wooded habitats. Within these habitats, the leopard rat snake finds coolness and seclusion in fencerows, ruins, and old stone walls.

Diet: Temperatures that are too hot or too cold may inhibit feeding by these snakes. Like many of the small and slender rat snakes of the world, *Z. situla* prefers small meals of nestling rodents and ground-dwelling birds. Hatchlings and juveniles often eagerly accept lizards and tree frogs. Until well acclimated, leopard rat snakes may prefer live wild mice—such as white-footed or deer mice—over laboratory mice. If providing wild mice would be a problem for you, find out about the prey preferences of any leopard rat snakes you intend to acquire. If taken from the wild these snakes may bear rather heavy loads of endoparasites that will require purging.

Temperature: Leopard rat snakes do not tolerate excessive warmth well. Their terrarium should be large enough to allow the snakes to thermoregulate. A daytime hot spot of 82 to 85°F (28–29°C) should be provided on one end of the terrarium but the rest of the cage should be several degrees cooler. Night temperatures may be allowed to fall by several degrees.

Reproduction: Leopard rat snakes breed following their emergence from hibernation. Males seem especially stimulated by the scent of the female's post emergence skin shedding. Once the snakes breed, the female will lay anywhere from 2 to 8 (usually 3 to 5) eggs. The hatchlings measure just under a foot (30 cm) in length and feed after their postnatal shed. Some eat newly born domestic mice, but many prefer the pinkies of wild mouse and vole species.

Availability: Because of their great beauty and comparative rarity, leopard rat snakes are coveted by collectors. Expensive even in Europe, the few Imports that reach the United States may be almost prohibitively costly. This beautiful and interesting species is now being bred by few American hobbyists.

Some Asian Favorites

Because of the initial, and sometimes, continued, defensiveness and the perceived delicacy of many of these species, Asian rat snakes were long overlooked and underappreciated by American herpetoculturists. However, it was on already languishing wild-collected examples that many of our perceptions were based. Such problems as endoparasite loads, dehydration, hunger, and shipping stress were behind the perceived delicacy of many of these snakes.

Fortunately, our increased knowledge of these snakes in the wild, better husbandry techniques, and better veterinary procedures have now allowed herpetoculturists to establish successful breeding programs.

Today (2006), many Asian rat snakes that were once almost unobtainable, are available for all hobbyists to enjoy. This isn't to say it's clear sailing when it comes to keeping all Asian rat snakes. A few taxa like the coveted Moellendorff's rat snake and the equally intriguing Mandarin rat snake have largely defied our efforts. But some progress is now being made even with those.

Although most of the Asian rat snakes are perfectly capable of constriction, many immobilize their prey by grasping it in their mouth, then throwing a single loop of their body over it. *C. radiata, O. taeniurus ridleyi,* and *Gonyosoma oxycephalum* use this method.

The Amur Rat Snakes:
North Amur Rat Snake
and South Amur Rat Snake
(*Elaphe schrencki* and *E. anomala*)

Appearance: An initial glance at the North Amur rat snake reminds most viewers of the eastern kingsnake. Adult *E. schrencki* are black snakes that are patterned with numerous pale crossbands. The labials are light, often a rather bright yellow with black scale seams. This brilliance carries over onto the chin and may be present subcaudally as well. The tail is often patterned beneath but may be immaculate (or largely so). The venter is also variable, being light in color and either heavily, sparsely, or virtually unpatterned. Hatchlings and juveniles are prominently marked with dark-edged dorsal saddles of some shade of brown, and tan to

The adult color of North Amur rat snakes, Elaphe schrencki, *(left) is very different from that of the juveniles.*

gray crossbars. Hatchlings look very like the adults of the more southerly *E. anomala*. A dark bar begins just posterior to the nostril, extends through the eye, and angles downward to the angle of the jaw.

Captive care: These gentle and powerful constrictors are hardy and easily kept, feeding on rodents. Most adults will tackle prey up to the size of medium rats.

Size: Both races of this snake frequently exceed 4 feet (1.2 m) in length and may occasionally attain a length of 6 feet (185 cm).

Temperature: Since they come from an area typified by harsh, cool weather, captive Amur rat snakes do not require a lot of auxiliary heat. A cage temperature of 72–76°F (22–24°C), which is provided with an illuminated basking spot of 82–85°F (27.7–29°C), is satisfactory.

Hibernation: As would be expected of a northern clime snake, hibernation is a necessary part of reproductive cycling. Although a hibernation of up to five months has been suggested, Amur rat snakes breed well (and regularly) with a standardized 90-day hibernation. Cooled to a temperature between 47 and 52°F (8.3–11°C), the snakes should be aroused for a drink at two to three week intervals.

Reproduction: Normally a clutch will contain from 7 to 16 eggs. One clutch of 30 eggs and another of 50—the latter from a dead female—have been reported.

Range: *Elaphe schrencki*, the more northerly of the two species, is found in Siberia, Manchuria, and northeastern Korea. It is replaced in western Korea to northeastern China by *E. anomala*.

Although it fades somewhat with age, adult (left) South Amur rat snakes, Elaphe anomala, retain the juvenile color and pattern.

The Other Species

The South Amur rat snake, *E. anomala*, was long considered a subspecies of *E. schrencki*. It has a ground color of tan, olive tan, or olive gray, which brightens posteriorly. The blotches are only vaguely darker and are edged on both leading and trailing margins with buff. The blotches are usually better defined (and darker) from a point two-thirds of the way back to the tailtip. Lip, chin, ventrals, and subcaudals are often a rich, unpatterned yellow. Hatchlings and juveniles are duller than those of *E. schrencki*.

Moellendorff's (or Copper-headed) Rat Snake

(*Orthriophis moellendorffi*)

In contrast to the hardiness of the preceding species, the equally large (6 feet [1.8 m] plus) *O. moellendorffi* has proven to be a delicate captive. As with many wild-collected rat snakes, the heavy parasite load borne by most individuals becomes a significant problem when the snake is stressed by capture and shipping. The mortality of some has been attributed to an irreversible buildup of caseous (cheesy) material in the lung, which may actually be evidence of an overwhelming infection. A very occasional specimen of this pretty rat snake of somewhat divergent appearance not only survives captivity but does well.

Moellendorff's rat snakes can vary in temperament. Some individuals never tolerate any sort of direct interaction with people but others will allow gentle handling.

Captive care: *Orthriophis moellendorffi* is a powerful and supple constrictor, preferring

Moellendorff's rat snake, **Orthriophis moellendorffi,** *is a difficult-to-acclimate Asian species.*

small prey items. Few specimens will accept domestic mice. Most of the few that do feed prefer rat pups, chicks, wild mice, and voles.

Temperature: Moellendorff's rat snakes seem to prefer cool weather and cool habitats, a preference that must be considered in captivity, along with the possibility of a very restricted diet. These snakes are forest-dwellers in southern China and adjacent northern Vietnam. Captives seem to do best when terrarium temperatures are maintained in the low to mid-70s°F (21–24°C). *Orthriophis moellendorffi* should be provided with an illuminated basking spot that is a few degrees warmer than the ambient temperature, which means 75°F (24°C).

Coloration: Although some specimens are duller than others, for the most part, *O. moellendorffi* is an attractive snake. Head coloration

may vary from dull copper to a rather bright orange-red. The head is broad temporally, the snout somewhat squared and elongate, and the overall conformation looks very much like that of the New World *Senticolis triaspis* (see page 80). The tail is red with broad, dark-edged maroon rings. The ground color is an attractive olive gray, gray, or silver gray (interstitial skin is lighter than the scales). The brown to reddish brown dorsal saddles and lateral blotches are usually dark edged. The dorsal saddles may have lighter centers, but usually do not. Light interstitial skin may be visible both in the ground area and blotches if the snakes are distended with food and/or are tightly coiled. Aberrant color morphs such as hypomelanism are known.

Availability: Inexpensive wild-collected Moellendorff's rat snakes are occasionally available. However, most wild examples rapidly succumb to a variety of health issues. A very few captive-bred examples are available each year. These are very expensive but by far the better choice.

Breeding: *O. moellendorffi* is seldom bred in captivity. Most of the very few captive-hatched specimens that become available are from eggs deposited by females that were gravid when imported. Strangely, however, no matter what time of year the snakes are imported, gravid females are seldom seen. This is in sharp contrast to virtually all other species of rat snakes. Eggs of this species are fairly large but the clutch size is small (4 to 11 eggs). Captive longevity of over 21 years has been reported by one zoo.

The Mandarin Rat Snake
(*Euprepiophis mandarinus*)

This gentle snake is another of rather atypical-appearing Asian rat snake. The head of *E. man-*

This Mandarin rat snake has a strangely diffuse pattern.

darinus is narrow and not well differentiated from the neck, while the snout is short and rounded.

Coloration: *E. mandarinus* is one of the least variable of the Asian rat snakes. The dorsal saddles are diamond-shaped with bright yellow centers. The black of the saddles may extend downward to the ventral plates and, in addition, there may be irregular black lateral markings. The head has black rostral markings, a black supraorbital bar connects the eyes, and a pair of black subocular triangles is present. An anteriorly directed black chevron appears on the rear of the head, bordered posteriorly by a yellow chevron. The yellow venter may be extensively spotted or crossbanded with black. The ground color may be olive fawn, pale gray, or olive gray. A few specimens have the dorsal blotches fragmented and broken; however, with these, it is the pattern, not the coloration, that is changed.

Size: Although *E. mandarinus* of slightly more than 5 feet (1.5 m) in total length are known, most are between 30 and 40 inches (76–101.6 cm) long.

Habits: *Euprepiophis mandarina* is a montane species found in northern Burma, northern Vietnam, and southern and eastern China. The first recorded specimens were found at altitudes above 2,000 feet (608 m) on forested slopes and plateaus. Additionally, *E. mandarinus* is preferentially crepuscular and nocturnal. Temperatures, especially night temperatures, are relatively cool and the humidity fairly high in such habitats.

Captive care: Captive specimens respond best to temperatures in the high 60s to mid-70s°F (20–24°C). Many captives show a reluctance to bask in brilliantly illuminated hot spots but will thermoregulate over a heat tape. The absolute warmest spot in their terrarium should reach 84°F (28.8°C). Even well-acclimated

Mandarin rat snakes may cease to feed if terrarium temperatures exceed 83°F (28°C).

The terrarium should always have hiding areas where the snakes may feel secure, as well as a container of barely moistened sphagnum so the snake can seek out a humid and secluded resting spot if desired; the container should be large enough for the snake to completely hide himself.

Wild-collected Mandarin rat snakes are difficult captives, often refusing food or regurgitating if they do eat. Postmortems usually reveal heavy parasite loads. Imported snakes should be wormed and then offered the smallest of meals. Some of these snakes prefer newly born rats over mice, while others will eagerly accept newly hatched button quail. Many will accept wild mice but refuse lab mice. Food items that are small in size are much less likely to be regurgitated.

Not only is the Mandarin rat snake, **Euprepiophis mandarinus,** *beautiful, it is also a difficult species to acclimate.*

Captive-hatched Mandarin rat snakes have proven much hardier, and far more expensive, than specimens taken from the wild. Captive-bred babies usually feed readily on lab mice. Recent research shows us that when a female snake can smell prey items that she is not accustomed to, her young are far more likely to consume those prey items—but they are still fragile captives.

We suggest that Mandarins rat snakes of any age and any birth site be kept by experienced keepers.

Behavior: Even the best-acclimated Mandarin rat snakes are secretive. They will burrow persistently in cypress bark mulch or dry, unmilled sphagnum moss.

Captives become stressed easily, and newly fed specimens will often regurgitate their meal if they are handled.

Breeding: Mandarin rat snakes are not easily cycled to reproductive readiness. The very few captive breedings that have been documented occurred after a 90-day period of hibernation.

Reproduction: A clutch consists of up to 8 eggs. Incubation takes from 45 to 58 days. Hatchlings are between 11 and 13 inches (27.9–33 cm) in length.

The Beauty Snakes (also called the Striped-Tailed Rat Snakes)
(*Orthriophis taeniurus*)

Many of the subspecies of this pretty snake are referred to simply as "beauty snakes," and indeed they are beautiful. This widespread Asian rat snake has at least seven identified subspecies and one (perhaps two) awaiting formal scientific description.

Taken individually, the habitats of the races of *O. taeniurus* vary considerably. Some sub-

The brightly colored Taiwan beauty snake, Orthriophis taeniura friesi, *is a hobbyist favorite.*

species are denizens of mountain fastnesses at elevations of 11,000 feet (3,344 m), while others occur near sea level.

Appearance: The races of *O. taeniurus* vary tremendously in external appearance. Some, such as the Chinese beauty snake, *O. t. taeniurus* and the Taiwan beauty snake, *O. t. friesi*, are proportionately heavy bodied, strongly blotched anteriorly, striped posteriorly, and have a ground color of olive buff to olive yellow-green. The yellow to reddish Ryukyu beauty snake, *O. t. schmackeri*, tends to be a little more attenuate, weakly blotched anteriorly, and more strongly so posteriorly. The posterior, light, middorsal stripe, if present, is frequently interrupted, or at least strongly encroached upon, by the posterior blotches.

Some subspecies, such as the Indonesian striped-tailed rat snake, *O. t. grabowskyi* and the cave striped-tailed rat snake, *O. t. ridleyi*, are whipsnake-slender, of light coloration, lack anterior blotches, and are cleanly striped for the posterior three-fifths of their length.

Both of these latter snakes are frequently found in or near caves and feed upon bats, which is one reason you rarely see these snakes offered by dealers. Mocquard's beauty snake, *O. t. mocquardi*, tends to be intermediate in appearance between the heavy, blotched forms and the attenuate racerlike subspecies.

The Yunnan striped-tailed rat snake, *O. t. yunnanensis*, has less well-defined anterior body blotches than other blotched forms.

A bluish colored form, not yet described, is known from Burma, and a second, equally blue and very similar, from Vietnam. The undescribed Vietnamese form is called the blue beauty snake. It has been available to American hobbyists since the late 1990s.

Size: Occasionally attaining a length of more than 8 feet (240 cm), *O. t. ridleyi* is so slender

Subspecies of E. taeniura	Number of ventrals	Range
friesei	240–260	Taiwan
grabowskyi	275–290	Borneo to Malaysia
mocquardi	251–264	Southern China to northern Vietnam
ridleyi	more than 280	Thailand to Sumatra
schmackeri	250–260	Ryukyu Islands
taeniurus	230–250	Thailand, Burma, southeastern China
yunnanensis	220–260	Northern Vietnam and adjacent China, including Yunnan Province
taeniurus ssp. 1	276–293	Burma
taeniurus ssp. 2	275–293	Vietnam

that even the longest individuals appear smaller than their actual size. The remaining subspecies are somewhat smaller when adult, attaining lengths of 5.5–7.75 feet (168–235 cm).

Captive care: Impressive size, beautiful colors, and intricate patterns make the various beauty snakes hobbyist favorites.—but the species is not always a trouble-free choice. As with many of the Old World rat snakes, wild-collected, imported *O. taeniurus* are often heavily parasitized and badly dehydrated. These are difficult to acclimate to captivity. However, captive-hatched babies are actually hardy, feed readily, and are easily handled.

The snakes are both crepuscular and nocturnal in their activity patterns, often actively prowling their cages in the evening after having spent the day secluded in their hide box. The snakes often remain hidden if there's considerable human activity outside their cage.

Beauty snakes seem most content when kept cool. Terrarium temperatures between 70 and 76°F (21–24°C) are satisfactory. An illuminated basking area with a temperature of about 86°F (30°C) may not be frequently used by the snakes. If you have acquired wild-collected examples, they should be purged of endoparasites before they are cooled for the winter or bred.

All races of the beauty snake accept mice of any age.

Breeding: *Orthriophis t. grabowski* and *O. t. schmackeri* are unknown or rare in American herpetoculture, but the other races are popular with hobbyists and are readily available. The Yunnan, Chinese, Taiwan, and Mocquard's beauty snakes are easily bred but the cave striped-tailed rat snake is a problematic breeder.

Some hobbyists prefer to hibernate their beauty snakes for a period of about two months. When hibernated they are kept in complete darkness, and roused every two weeks or so and allowed to drink. Other breeders choose to just cool the snakes for a similar duration. A natural photoperiod and ready access to drinking water is important for cooled snakes. A very successful breeder in southern Florida cools his specimens during the months of winter by opening the windows in his breeding facility. The falling night temperatures and shortened photoperiod seem to adequately cycle and stimulate his breeders.

Note: Fully hibernated snakes need no food; cooled snakes may require food, but more infrequently and of smaller size.

Orthriophis t. ridleyi seems to cycle best if fully hibernated, but even then the snakes do not always breed.

Eggs: Depending on the subspecies, size, age, and condition, females of the various beauty snakes deposit between 6 and 25 eggs. Incubation is somewhat more than 60 days at temperatures between 76 and 83°F (25–28°C). The hatchlings are robust and look like duller, smaller renditions of the adults. Hatchlings are 12 to 16 inches (30–40 cm) in length.

Note: The number of ventral scales of the various races of this species may differ widely from other races or may overlap. Although many of these counts are decades old and were made from a very limited number of specimens, this is still the best data available. All beauty snake data is badly in need of updating and some races perhaps reevaluated.

The Radiated (or Copperhead) Rat Snake

(*Coelognathus radiatus*)

Behavior: There could hardly be a more defensive colubrine species than wild-caught adults of this interesting and pretty Asian rat snake. When even vaguely threatened, the radiated (so called for the three dark lines that radiate outward from the eye) pulls its neck

Orthriophis taeniura ridleyi is one of the two strongly striped races of this species. It is called the cave rat snake.

back, inflates its throat, and vigorously defends itself. Since adults can exceed a 6-foot (1.8-m) length by several inches, the striking range is fairly extensive and very impressive. If possible, radiated rat snakes would prefer to avoid confrontation by fleeing. They are a fast-moving species, the flight actions more like that of a racer than of a typical rat snake.

Coloration: Unlike many of its Asian congenerics, the radiated rat snake is striped anteriorly rather than posteriorly. The four stripes—two heavy dorsolateral stripes and two more poorly defined lateral stripes—are of variable length and best defined on the anterior trunk. Striping may fade by midbody or continue almost to the tail. The ground color of *C. radiatus* is also variable, from buff, tan, light

Albino radiated rat snakes are now quite common.

brown, or coppery russet, to yellowish or greenish. The three dark stripes radiating from the eye, and the dark collar, with which the uppermost of the orbital stripes connects, are diagnostic of the species. Hypomelanistic (lacking much melanin), anerythristic (lacking all red pigment), and albino specimens of the radiated rat snake are known.

Breeding: All color morphs of this pretty and active rat snake are now captive bred in fair numbers. Few wild-collected snakes are imported. Hibernation is not necessary to cycle the radiated rat snake for breeding but a period of winter cooling is beneficial. Healthy adult females will multi-clutch and up to four clutches a season have been recorded. A clutch consists of two to six eggs. An incubation temperature of 79 to 83°F (27–29°C) should be maintained. The hatchlings are small, often less than 10 inches (25 cm) in overall length, and will usually readily accept prekilled pinky mice.

Easily seen in this portrait, the radiated rat snake derives its names from the radiating facial lines.

The radiated rat snake, Coelognathus radiatus, is often defensive and quite ready to bite.

Diet: Some wild-collected *C. radiatus* can be problematic feeders. Housing them in sizable, quiet terraria with ample hiding spots and varying the prey—even the color of the prey—may help overcome their reluctance to eat. When a mouse is refused, a small rat, a baby chick, or quail may be accepted.

The Chinese King and the Steppes Rat Snakes

The Chinese King Rat Snake
(*Elaphe carinata*)

"Stinking Goddess" and "Chinese Stink Snake" are two names used by American dealers for the variable but often very pretty, *E. carinata*. The names refer to this snake's remarkably large musk glands and an extraordinary ability to produce scent when it is defensive. However, king rat snakes are not usually any more prone to "musk" than many other rat snake species. This heavy-bodied and often defensive snake attains a length of 8 feet (2.1 m). With frequent gentle handling some examples (especially captive-born babies) become tractable.

Coloration: Three subspecies of the king rat snake are recognized, but the snake is so variable that subspecific recognition is all but impossible. Besides its natural variability of pattern and color, the king rat snake undergoes marked ontogenetic changes. Hatchling and juvenile specimens are quite dull, the ground color often being a pale olive brown or an equally pale olive green.

Obscure to rather well-defined crossbands and/or variable spotting are usually present on juvenile specimens. The banding tends to be strongest anteriorly and the spotting most prevalent posteriorly. The ground color darkens with growth until some specimens become an inky black, while others merely become a darker olive. Those black specimens usually develop a brilliant yellow spot in the center of most scales while retaining a hint of the anterior banding. The edges of the scales and interstitial skin remains black. Snakes of this phase are remarkably beautiful. The olive-colored adults develop white and black interstitial skin anteriorly, retain light anterior banding, and, unless upset and inflated, appear rather unicolored posteriorly. Actually, the posterior interstitial skin is dark and shows best when the snake is in a defensive posture or distended with food.

The Chinese king rat snake, Elaphe carinata, can attain a length of over 8 feet (2.1 m).

A portrait of a pretty Chinese king rat snake.

Unlike most rat snakes, the vast majority of which have round pupils, at least some specimens of *E. carinata* have teardrop-shaped pupils. This divergent pupil shape is most noticeable when the snakes are in bright light.

Range and availability: The Chinese king rat snake ranges from eastern China to the Ryukyu Islands. It is now being bred in the United States in small numbers. It is a relatively inexpensive species.

Behavior: When fully defensive, *Elaphe carinata* epitomizes the word "belligerent." When frightened, the snake raises its head and neck well above the ground, inflates its neck and anterior body, assumes an S curve, strikes, and bites. A bite from a large individual can be painful but is not of serious consequences.

Diet: This divergent Asian rat snake has a varied diet. It will eat not only the typical mammals and birds, but also frogs, toads, lizards, baby turtles, turtle eggs, and other snakes. Cannibalism is well documented; if more than one king rat snake is kept to a cage, it is therefore very important to have all of similar size.

Breeding: This is not a difficult species to breed. A large terrarium or cage with hiding areas, a steady diet of rodents, and a two- to three-month-long period of hibernation should enable you to cycle and breed these snakes. Breeding occurs in the spring after the snake's emergence from hibernation.

Breeding can be rough, with the male immobilizing the female by biting her on the back of the head and nape. A clutch normally contains from 5 to 10 eggs, but up to 15 have been documented. Incubate at 80 to 83°F (26–29°C) for 40 to 60 days.

Although some hatchlings will accept rodent prey, many insist on lizards for their first few meals. Scenting a mouse with lizard feces or blood may induce an otherwise reluctant snake to accept the rodent.

The Steppes Rat Snake
(*Elaphe dione*)

Although the hatchlings and occasional Steppes adults (particularly those of Chinese origin) can be attractive, most adult Steppes rat snakes are not colorful. Despite its somewhat uninspired color and pattern, this snake is now being bred by several American breeders and hobbyists. It has a gentle disposition and is still far more commonly seen in European collections than those in America.

The Steppes rat snake attains an adult size of from 30 to about 36 inches (76–91 cm) in length. Those with the most attractive patterns look at first glance like a twin-spotted rat snake, *E. bimaculata*, having a yellowish ground color with well-defined strawberry spots or dark stripes. Others have an unpatterned olive green to brownish red dorsum, or have a dark ground color and barely visible spots or stripes.

Although not brightly colored, the Japanese rat snake, **Elaphe climacophora,** *is a favorite of many hobbyists.*

Range: The range of the Steppes rat snake extends over most of central Asia. It may be encountered from near sea level to rather high elevations, and is rather generally recognized as an important predator of rodents.

Hibernation: The Steppes rat snake requires a lengthy period of hibernation to induce reproductive cycling. A period of 80 to 100 days is suggested. When the snakes are active, provide a natural photoperiod to keep their reproductive timing on schedule.

Breeding may occur in the fall, prior to hibernation or following the snake's emergence from hibernation in the spring. Those females bred in the fall retain viable sperm and lay fertile eggs in the spring. Springtime breeding activity seems to take place after the female's posthibernation skin shedding. Similar to many northern latitude rat snakes, development within the egg is rapid, with the young pipping the eggs two to three weeks after deposition. Incubation temperature should be 82°F (28°C). Soon after hatching—sometimes before their posthatching shed—hatchlings are ready to feed. Pinky mice are usually readily accepted.

The Japanese Rat Snake
(*Elaphe climacophora*)

The normal morph of this nervous snake is readily available in the United States from specialty breeders. The albino morph is less frequently seen and more expensive.

Coloration: This rat snake is not at all colorful. The ground color can vary from the dullest of olive gray to a reasonably bright olive yellow-green. The most consistent single marking is a dark postorbital bar that extends downward from the eye to the angle of the mouth. Some adults bear vague saddles; some bear two to four vague lines; others (especially young adults) combine the two. If only two lines are present, it is the dorsolateral pair. If four lines are present, the dorsolateral pair is the better defined.

Hatchlings and juveniles are like the adults, but with slightly better-defined patterns. In Japan, the albino phase—called the Shirohebi—is rigidly protected. It occurs in the wild in fair numbers, in the vicinity of the city of Iwakuni, Japan. Albino hatchlings bear traces of saddles; the adult snakes are red-eyed and a unicolored pinkish white. Because of untold generations of inbreeding, even wild specimens demonstrate abnormalities in scalation as well as abnormally large eyes. Despite being lauded as a national treasure, the population of wild albinos has been subjected to illegal collecting. Their numbers are rapidly being depleted.

Elaphe climacophora is well known and readily tolerated in its native Japan. It is recognized immediately as an important predator of mice and rats. Perhaps because of this tolerance, the snake is said to be relatively common, even near human habitations.

Besides rodents, captives accept birds and their eggs.

Size and breeding: Adults may measure 5 feet (1.5 m). Females seem to mature somewhat more slowly than the males. This species seldom becomes sexually active until its third or fourth year of life.

Reproduction: A 90-day hibernation and a natural photoperiod are needed to cycle this rat snake. Older and larger females are more reliable breeders and produce more and larger eggs than younger examples. Clutches can number from 3 to 18 eggs, with between 10 and 13 being the norm. The eggs of this species will incubate successfully at temperatures between 78 and 82°F (26–28°C). Incubation takes from 58 to 70 days. Hatchlings are 12 to 15 inches (30–38 cm) long.

Captive care: The Japanese rat snake is a heavy-bodied species that is quite terrestrial in its habits. Although not overly active, these snakes should be housed in a fairly large terrarium or cage that contains several hiding areas; cockatiel nesting boxes, corkbark tubes, or dedicated plastic snake hiding boxes of various sizes seem to work equally well.

Hatchlings are large enough to accept a fuzzy baby mouse; adult Japanese rat snakes are entirely capable of eating prekilled rats of moderate size.

The Common Trinket Rat Snake

(*Coelognathus helenae*)

Another of the Asiatic rat snakes, the common trinket rat snake has been long popular in Europe. It is slowly but surely gaining popularity in the United States.

Coloration: Like many other rat snakes, the common trinket rat snake (or merely trinket snake, as it is referred to by most hobbyists), *C. helenae* is variably hued. While the darker specimens may not be considered pretty, those on the lighter end of the spectrum (buff to yellow) are quite beautiful. At first glance, the coloration of these is reminiscent of a blonde phase Trans-Pecos rat snake, *Bogertophis s. subocularis* (see page 78).

The head of the trinket rat snake is usually patternless except for a dark suture between the two parietal scales and a dark (and variably discernible) postocular stripe. A pair of elongate

Coelognathus helenae *is commonly referred to as the trinket rat snake.*

dark nape stripes is almost invariably present, and is echoed with a second, ventrolateral pair. The body pattern, more difficult to describe, must necessarily be divided into anterior and posterior categories. Anteriorly (but posterior to the neck stripes), the trinket rat snake bears irregularly edged, dark dorsal blotches. Dorso-laterally in these dark blotches are thin, even darker vestiges of striping. Laterally, the dark blotches often contain irregular light scales that, together, form a small light blotch. Poste-riorly, the blotches become obscure and the dorsum often lightens; however, the flanks darken in an evenly but obscurely edged, broad lateral stripe. The venter is light and, if marked at all, is only lightly and irregularly clouded.

Size: This is a small- to medium-sized rat snake with a proportionately slender body. The adult length averages 3 to 4 feet (0.9–1.2 m), sometimes reaching 5 feet (1.5 m). Males are slightly smaller than females.

Range: The trinket snake ranges over most of the Indian subcontinent, eastward to Nepal, and southward to Sri Lanka.

Breeding: Because of its basically tropical distribution, brumation is not needed for breed-ing. A simple cooling period is all that is needed to assure success in most cases, and successful breedings of this species abound with no winter cooling at all. Like many tropical rat snakes, *C. helenae* will multi-clutch in the course of each season. Needless to say, only those breeders in very good condition should undergo multi-clutching.

Clutches typically number from four to seven eggs and, at 82–86°F (28–30°C); a normal incu-bation period is about 60 days.

Diet: Hatchlings will usually feed eagerly on newly born mice.

Behavior: Although newly collected wild specimens will readily bite, once acclimated, this is a quiet and easily handled rat snake. It is

Twin-spotted rat snakes, Elaphe bimaculata, *may be either spotted (left) or striped.*

easy to see why breeders who work with the trinket rat snake become so enamored of it.

Two Look-alike Chinese Rat Snake Species

The Chinese Twin-spotted Rat Snake

The Chinese twin-spotted rat snake, *Elaphe bimaculata*, is a very typical but interesting little rat snake.

Range and description: This 28- to 36-inch (71–91-cm) rat snake is now being bred in fair numbers by American hobbyists. It has two distinctly different morphs, one having two rows of spots down its back—and the morph for which the species is named—and the other being prominently striped. There seems a tendency for the striped phase to have a darker

ground color and less contrasting markings than those normally seen on the light morph. The twin-spotted phase of *E. bimaculata* is quite attractive. The dorsolateral spots are often discrete anteriorly but may be joined across the back posteriorly.

There is a stylized spearpoint on the crown, the ends of which extend backward onto the neck as short stripes. Dark postorbital stripes begin at the angle of the mouth, pass diagonally upward through each eye where they narrow, and continue as a dark, sometimes interrupted, line around the tip of the snout. Another marking, which passes over the top of the snout, connects the eyes.

Lateral spots may be bold or poorly defined and may be discrete or joined, forming an irregular stripe. The striped phase is just that— prominently patterned with two dorsolateral

The red-backed rat snake, Oocatophus rufodorsatus, *is another Asian species that may be either spotted (bottom) or striped.*

and two lateral stripes. Vestiges of the spots often remain visible in each of the dorsolateral stripes.

Hibernation: It has been found that hibernation and a natural photoperiod is necessary to breed these northern latitude rat snakes. A three-month period of hibernation is suggested. Hibernation temperatures as low as 49°F (10°C) and as high as 59°F (16°C) have proven success-

ful. Copulation may occur prior to, or following hibernation.

Breeding: Fall breedings have resulted in fertile eggs being deposited the following spring with no other breedings having occurred. Clutches of the twin-spot are small (three to eight eggs) and eggs are large. The incubation duration is a typical northern latitude-style abbreviation, varying from three to four weeks. Hatchlings are 9 to 11 inches (22.8–27.9 cm) long and are duller than, but otherwise quite similar to, their parents. They brighten up as they mature.

Diet: Newly born mice are usually eagerly accepted by the hatchling snakes.

The Red-backed Rat Snake
(*Oocatochus rufodorsatus*)

Appearance: In pattern and coloration this little rat snake is very like *Elaphe bimaculata*, but because it bears three dorsal stripes it can also be likened to an eastern garter snake. It derives its common name from the literal translation of *rufodorsatus*.

The dorsal ground color may be tan, gray, or rufous. The top of the head bears an intricate, dark, anteriorly directed spearpoint. A dark chevron, either entire or interrupted at the point, again anteriorly directed, connects the eyes. The dorsal (vertebral) pattern usually consists of a single, broad, prominent, dark-edged light stripe that runs from nape to tail tip. The two broad dark stripes that border the vertebral stripe may be whole or broken into a series of elongate blotches.

The sides are pale and may bear a row of irregular blotches. The sides may be as prominent as the pale vertebral stripe or pale and poorly defined. The belly is marked with irregular dark blotches and smudges.

Size: The adult size of this rat snake is 18 to 26 inches (45.7–66 cm). The largest known specimen was 36 inches (91 cm) long. These are interesting and hardy little snakes, but in many ways, diet among them, they are quite unlike other rat snakes.

Range: The red-backed rat snake is a semi-aquatic species that is most common near rice paddies or other quiet waters. It ranges northward from southeastern China through the Korean Peninsula.

Reproduction: Once purged of endoparasites, the imported adults of this little snake do well in captivity. Because adults are small at adulthoood, three to four red-backed rat snakes can be housed in a 20-gallon (76-L) terrarium.

This rat snake has been bred in captivity on numerous occasions. Unlike all other rat snakes, *Oocatochus* bears live young. A clutch contains from 3 to 25 tiny babies that are only about 4½ inches (11 cm) in total length. Although most success has been achieved when the adult snakes are hibernated, a few clutches have been born to adults that have not. Most reported hibernations have been about 90 days in length.

Diet: Although some hatchling red-backed rat snakes will accept the tiniest of pinky mice, most of them prefer a diet of fish, and it's easy to find small guppies or other feeder fish small enough for a 4½-inch (11-cm) snakelet. Some hatchlings will accept insects such as crickets or small grasshoppers as well. In these cosmopolitan dietary preferences, *Oocatochus rufodorsatus* also differs from other rat snakes.

This little rat snake still seems much more popular in Europe than in the United States, but the interest gap is now closing.

The Asian Red-tailed Green Rat Snake
(*Gonyosoma oxycephalum*)

Called the red-tailed green rat snake no matter what color its tail happens to be, most examples of this beautiful snake still are wild-collected individuals. However, a few clutches are produced annually by hobbyists and breeders. The species has an immense range and is of very variable coloration.

Coloration: Typically, specimens from tropical Thailand, Sumatra, and Sabah are of some shade of green (often leaf-green) with a tail of orange, red, or blue. The red coloration is brightest in the center of each scale, the sutures being paler red to gray. The supralabial (upper lip) scales are usually much brighter than the dorsal surface of the head. A dark eye stripe separates the two colors. The ventral coloration is usually paler (more yellowish) than the green of the back and sides.

Specimens from Java may be pearl gray, without a strongly contrastingly colored tail, and have a mottled yellow to mottled green and yellow or solid gray head. The dorsal and lateral scales are darkest on the trailing edge,

Gonyosoma oxycephalum, the red-tailed green rat snake, is actually one of the most variably colored of the commonly seen Asian rat snakes.

often having an interesting and beautiful scalloped look.

From other areas of the range, such as Celebes and surrounding islands, the ground color may be a warm tan, buff, or olive brown. The tail may be gray to black or lack contrasting colors. The head is usually tinged with yellow or pale green and a dark eye stripe is present. The lower sides of the body and venter are somewhat lighter than the back.

Captive care: Because most wild-collected red-tails are heavily parasitized and are badly dehydrated by the time they get to pet dealers, they have been classically one of the more difficult snakes to acclimate; bluntly, that means the vast majority of them die. Upper respiratory ailments are also commonly encountered in these wild-caught snakes, compounding whatever health problems they arrive with.

On the rare occasions when reasonably healthy red-tails are received, by immediately purging them of their parasite load and rehydrating them, some may be saved. Because wild-collected specimens are so difficult to acclimate, the very few captive-bred red-tailed rat snakes that become available are relatively expensive.

Hatchlings: Most of the hatchlings currently offered are from incubated eggs laid by imported gravid females. Reported clutches are small, numbering from three to nine rather large, elongate eggs. The slender babies are from

Most color morphs of the red-tailed green rat snake have a bright yellow throat.

15 to 19 inches (38–48 cm) in length at emergence. The hatchlings are similar to, but duller than, the adults, especially prior to their postnatal shed. Although wild hatchlings reportedly feed on lizards and frogs, those that are captive hatched readily accept pinky mice as prey.

Range: *Gonyosoma oxycephalum* is a highly arboreal species. They should be kept in a spacious cage with sufficient height and branches on which to climb. Under such conditions these snakes will usually ascend to the top of the cage and loosely coil atop the highest branch.

Wild specimens have been found in trees and shrubs, often quite close to the water. In some areas *G. oxycephalum* frequents mangroves and is closely associated with brackish and salt water.

Behavior: In both appearance and demeanor, *Gonyosoma oxycephalum* is more racer-like than rat snake-like. Long—often to 8.5 feet (2.58 m), occasionally longer—slender snakes with narrow, but distinct, heads and proportionately long noses, this snake is fast, alert, and very defensive. Many wild-collected specimens steadfastly and vigorously resist handling. Stress-free management is important. Provide this species with secure hiding areas in the form of bird nesting boxes or corkbark tubes affixed near the top of the cage. Consider covering the front of the cage so the snake doesn't have to look at you or anything else it might consider alarming.

Temperature: A low-altitude tropical snake, the red-tail prefers warm temperatures and high humidity. Low cage humidity will often result in shedding problems. A night temperature of 75°F (24°C) and day temperatures of 86 to 90°F (30–32°C) are suitable. A natural photoperiod should be provided.

Note: Since this snake can be a difficult captive, it should be considered only by advanced hobbyists or zoological institutions.

Three "New" Rat Snakes

In the late 1990s, three diverse species of rat snakes became available to American hobbyists. These were the exquisitely beautiful, leaf-green

Asian green rat snake, *Elaphe prasina* (placed in the genus I by some taxonomists), the quietly colored but interesting Celebes black-tailed rat snake, *Gonyosoma janseni*, and several subspecies of the flamboyantly pretty bamboo rat snake, *Oreophis porphyraceus*. The green and the bamboo rat snakes are occasionally referred to as trinket snakes by some hobbyists.

Wild-collected examples of all of these species can be difficult to acclimate but captive-hatched specimens seem rather easily kept.

When these rat snakes first appeared on the pet trade, all were prohibitively expensive. However, each year the price of them has dropped a bit. At this time (2006) these snakes are still far too expensive to be considered pet store items, but all are available from specialty dealers and breeders at herp expos and at on-line reptile sales sites.

Green Bush Rat Snake

(*Elaphe prasina*)

Appearance: This is an arboreal rat snake of moderate size and slender build. The dorsal color is brilliant leaf green, occasionally with a bluish sheen. The belly is also green but a bit paler than the dorsum. The ventral coloration is separated from the dorsal coloration by a very thin white line along the outer edges of the ventral scutes. A vestige of a darker line may pass through the eye to the rear of the head. Traces of dark and light bars on the interstitial skin can actually be prominent if the snake is distended with food or heavily gravid.

Hatchlings are usually quite like the adults in overall color (some are slightly olive in color), but narrow bands of black, most prominent anteriorly, are very visible. Adults attain a length of about 4 feet (120 cm). The tongue is

When inflated with air or distended with food, the light interstitial skin of the Asian green bush rat snake is visible.

light brown. The undersurface of the tail and the tail tip may be terra-cotta.

Other than the olive tone of some hatchlings, no color variations are known. No subspecies have been described.

Range: The green bush rat snake ranges eastward from eastern India to western China and southward throughout Malaysia. It is often associated with montane habitats, but a few examples have now been found at low elevations.

Reproduction: *Elaphe prasina* does not seem difficult to breed. Throughout the spring, summer, and fall a daytime temperature of from 78–86°F (74–30°C) is suggested, with a nighttime drop of a few degrees. Although hibernation does not seem to be necessary, reproductive cycling may be aided by decreasing the cage

Oreophis porphyraceus coxi, the Thai bamboo rat snake, is certainly one of the most spectacular of this group.

temperature a few degrees during the winter. Relative humidity should be 65–85% year-round.

Most breeders separate the sexes for winter cooling, placing them together again when the terrarium temperatures are elevated in late February or early March. Breeding often follows a day or so later, especially if the female has recently shed. Clutches contain between three and nine eggs.

Diet: Hatchling *E. prasina* will usually readily accept newly born lab mice.

Bamboo Rat Snake

(*Oreophis porphyraceus*)

Appearance: There is probably no Asiatic rat snake that is more variable in color or pattern than this species, and there may be no other that is as poorly known and understood. There seems to be at least six subspecies and few of these races have stabilized patterns.

For example, the Thai race, *O. p. coxi*, usually bears two prominent dorsolateral stripes, but there are examples that are some combination of stripes and bands. This also holds true of the races *nigrofasciatus, kawakamii,* and *pulchra. Oreophis p. hainana* seems to be a primarily striped race while most *O. p. porphyraceus* are banded.

When stripes are present they are dorsolateral, narrow, precisely delineated, and usually unbroken. When bands are present they are dark, broad, and narrowly edged by even borders of white, black, or darker red.

On all races the dorsal ground color may vary from a rich vermillion, to brown, with tan, burnished copper, or purplish red, being common intermediate colors. Hatchlings and juveniles are the brightest and have the most strongly contrasting band and stripe colors. The oldest snakes are usually the dullest with the least contrast.

Because of this variability of pattern and color and the fact that the paper trail that would help you identify these snakes is usually nonexistent in the pet trade, it is best to acquire your bamboo rat snakes from an established and reputable breeder and rely on the identification provided.

Adding to the confusion is the variability of common names. Some races of the bamboo rat snake are referred to as mountain rat snakes or trinket snakes. All will bite readily if disturbed and some may strike and bite several times in rapid sequence.

Size: The adult size of all races is about 3 feet (90 cm) but occasional examples may near 4 feet (120 cm).

Range: In one or the other of its subspecies, *O. porphyraceus* ranges southward from central China and northern India to Sumatra.

Reproduction: Little is known about the reproductive cycling requirements of these snakes. What little is known has been derived primarily from observations made on captive pairs of *O. p. coxi*, the most commonly seen captive race.

Whether or not a period of hibernation is actually necessary to cycle this snake is conjectural. It is probable that examples from the southern portion of the range do not require an actual hibernation. But with that said, some breeders do hibernate their bamboo rat snakes and feel that this period of enforced dormancy enhances breeding potential. The length of the period of hibernation varies from 90 to 120 days.

These snakes are usually seen to breed following their first skin-shedding after emerging from hibernation.

A healthy adult female can produce several clutches of two to ten eggs annually. A clutch normally contains from three to five eggs. (The maximum number of clutches reportedly produced by a female in a single season is seven!)

Hatchlings are about 10 inches (25 cm) in length.

Sulawesi Black-tailed Rat Snake
(*Gonyosoma janseni*)

Appearance: The common name of the black-tailed rat snake is very appropriate for the normal phase of this slender arboreal snake. The ground color of the dorsum is olive tan to olive green and the posterior quarter to one third of the body is jet black. The black tail color may actually extend further forward on the sides than on the back and may form diagonal black lateral bars. A dark bar extends through each eye. The belly is yellowish anteriorly, usually darker at midbody and black posteriorly. The interstitial skin is black. Hatchlings are a dark olive green with a busy, dark herringbone pattern that extends far down the sides.

A melanistic phase is known and is now being bred in captivity. It is jet black with gray to olive green upper labial (lip) scales.

There are no described subspecies.

Behavior: When *G. janseni* is in a defensive mode, the tongue, which is black with blue edges, may be extended and held out for several seconds. At that time the throat and neck are inflated and expanded downward in an impressive threat display. Wild examples will not hesitate to strike and bite. Captive-hatched examples are much less apt to indulge in defensive tactics.

Size: The adult length of this shiny-scaled, whiplike (and sometimes nervous) snake is between 6 and 7½ feet (180–200 cm).

Range: The black-tailed rat snake is known only from the Indonesian island of Sulawesi (formerly Celebes).

Tropical rat snakes may be banded or not, but are usually black and yellow.

The Not-Really Rat Snake Rat Snakes

The snakes in the following three genera are actually more closely allied to the racers than to the rat snakes. They are included here because hobbyists often refer to them as rat snakes.

The Tropical Rat Snake
(*Spilotes pullatus*)

The various subspecies of this neotropical snake are slender, attenuate arborealists. Although pretty, they are often bad-tempered. Even healthy, long-term captive specimens may have a malnourished, keeled-back appearance. They are usually rather heavily parasitized when imported.

Range and coloration: *Spilotes pullatus* ranges in one of five subspecies from tropical Mexico through South America to northern Mexico. Most specimens are black snakes that are variably banded or speckled with yellow. In some cases, the coloration is reversed and the snake may be primarily yellow with black bands or speckles. Occasionally, solid black specimens, and, even more rarely, solid yellow specimens, are encountered. The snakes with a higher yellow to black ratio are more popular with hobbyists.

Reproduction: As with most other tropical rat snakes, *G. janseni* cycles easily for breeding. They require only warm summer temperatures—a daytime temperature of from 78–86°F (24–30°C) with a drop of a few degrees at night is suitable—a slight winter cooling, a natural photoperiod, and a relatively high terrarium humidity (65–85% is suggested during the warm months, a bit lower in winter). Most breeders separate the sexes during the winter and place them together again in the early spring. Breeding often occurs within a day or so after the reintroduction of the snakes but is most certain following the spring shedding of the female. Clutches contain between three and six eggs.

Hatchling *G. janseni* will usually readily accept newly born lab mice. Hatchlings are a very slender 16 to 18 inches (40–46 cm) in length.

Behavior and size: *Spilotes pullatus* is actually more closely related to the racers than to the rat snakes, and some behaviors reflect this. When frightened, the tropical rat snakes inflate their throats (vertically), draw back into a loose striking "S," and defend themselves through repeated strikes. They can near 10 feet (3 m) in length, so their striking range is quite memorable. It is an agile and active climber that ranges over a quite extensive home territory.

This is a broad-banded tropical rat snake from Suriname.

Although they may descend to the ground, if frightened the tropical rat snake will attempt to ascend into shrubs or trees.

Caging and temperature: Once acclimated, the tropical rat snakes is a hardy captive. This active snake does require a sizable, vertically oriented cage. The cage should be equipped with numerous horizontal limbs. Daytime temperatures should be from 80 to 90°F (27–33°C). Cage humidity should be high (a vining plant or two will help increase humidity and provides a hiding area for the snake) and ample fresh drinking water should be provided. Nighttime temperatures can be allowed to drop by a few degrees.

Feeding habits: This snake is not a constrictor. It grasps its prey in its strong jaws and immobilizes it by throwing a loop of its body over it. Opportunistic feeders, these snakes eat birds, amphibians, and other reptiles in addition to rodents.

Breeding: This species is now being bred with some regularity. Clutches contain from 6 to 17 eggs. The hatchlings are long (16 to 20 inches [40.6–50.8 cm]) and slender, and feed readily on small mice. Hatchlings are mini-replicas of the adults.

The Diadem Snakes
(*Spalerosophis* sp.)

The taxonomy of this genus is in disarray but it probably contains six species. Of those, only three are in hobbyist collections on any sort of basis and one of those three, *S. arenarius*, the blotched diadem snake, is very rarely seen. The two more commonly seen are the royal diadem snake, *S. atriceps*, and the Egyptian diadem snake, *S. diadema cliffordi*.

The Egyptian diadem snake is known scientifically as **Spalerosophis diadema cliffordi**.

The members of this genus are quite probably closely related to the racers. However, unlike the slender-bodied racers, the diadem snakes are rather heavy bodied. They are diurnally active, terrestrial, aridland snakes of the Middle

East, northern Africa, and central Asia, where, during the summer, very hot daytime temperatures are the norm.

Diadem rat snakes tend to be defensive bluffers, inflating their body, hissing and feinting when frightened. Some examples bite, most don't, and even those that do usually become tractable with time and gentle handling.

Feeding habits: The various diadem rat snakes are "search and overpower" hunters like the racers, rather than "wait and ambush" hunters like the rat snakes. Although the diadem snakes can constrict, they are less efficient at this than the true rat snakes. As often as not, the various diadem rat snakes will grasp a prey item, then immobilize it by throwing a single loop of their body over the creature. Diadem rat snakes have powerful jaws and the bite of a large specimen can rather quickly suffocate a small rodent. Juveniles also eat lizards.

The royal diadem snake, **Spalerosophis atriceps,** *is a hobbyist favorite.*

Spalerosophis arenarius, the blotched diadem snake, is a beautiful species that is occasionally available in the pet trade.

Coloration: The diadem snakes blend remarkably well with the desert sands on which they are found. Most of these snakes have sandy-tan to rich buff ground colors with large to small, darker saddles or blotches.

The blotched diadem snake has warm brown-to-strawberry markings against a sand-colored ground color. This Pakistan serpent attains a length of about 5.5 feet (165 cm).

The royal diadem snake is usually a richer color than its blotched relative, adults being buff to terra-cotta with black markings. Juveniles are of a lighter ground color than the adults and prominently saddled. There is a tendency for the neck markings to elongate to broken stripes (especially dorsolaterally) or attenuate blotches. The heads of some bear intricate patterns—the "diadem" markings from which the name is derived—while the heads of other specimens are

so dark that patterns are all but obscured. Adult length maxes out at about 5.5 feet (165 cm). It is a desert dweller found in India, Pakistan, and surrounding countries.

A portrait of a pair of northern tropical rat snakes, Spilotes pullatus mexicana.

The royal diadem may display impressively when first acquired, but quiets with time and gentler handling. It is now bred in fair numbers by both American and European hobbyists.

The third species, the Egyptian diadem, is olive buff to sandy buff with rather uniform-sized darker dorsal blotches. It attains a length of about 5.5 feet (165 cm), although most are smaller.

Captive care: If kept dry and warm, diadem rat snakes are hardy captives. Daytime temperatures of from 84 to 90° F (28–33°C) seem adequate. One end of the terrarium can be heated slightly by using an under-tank heating device. Nighttime temperatures can be allowed to drop by several degrees.

Reproduction: While a simple winter cooling and reduced photoperiod may reproductively cycle specimens from the southernmost reaches of the range, more northerly specimens may require an actual period of hibernation. Since

The common bird snake, **Pseustes poecilonotus,** *is prominently banded when young.*

it is usually impossible to determine the origin of a given specimen once it has entered the pet trade, those who wish to breed diadem rat snakes of any type usually opt for the period of full hibernation.

There are a few general guidelines to follow:

✔ Male diadem rat snakes often attain sexual maturity at an earlier age than females. They are capable of breeding at two to three years of age while the females, three to four years of age.

✔ Large females produce from four to ten large eggs and the hatchlings are from 16 to 18 inches (40–46 cm) in length at hatching.

✔ The young are similar to the adults in pattern but have duller colors.

Bird Snakes
(*Pseustes* sp.)

Besides being referred to as rat snakes, the members of the neotropical genus *Pseustes* are called bird snakes or puffing snakes. Of the four species in the genus only two appear in the American pet trade; these are the giant bird snake, *P. sulphureus*, and the common bird snake, *P. poecilonotus*.

All four genera are semiarboreal. Although bird snakes may be encountered on the ground, they are even more often seen in trees. If surprised while on the ground they escape by rapidly ascending nearby shrubs, vines, or trees. These snakes are seldom bred in captivity but wild-collected examples are available.

The reference to rats and birds in the common name pertains, of course, to the prey species these snakes are known to accept. The reference to puffing is derived from the snake's defensive behavior; when frightened, the snakes vertically

Although quietly colored, the common bird snake is a pretty, but defensive, species.

inflate their throat, hiss (puff) loudly, and strike viciously, typical frightened snake behavior.

Behavior: If there is a single trait that typifies the members of this genus, it is their defensive behavior. Big *Pseustes* can bite firmly and painfully and, if carelessly restrained, will not hesitate to do so. When an adult giant bird snake, *P. sulphureus*, rises in a defensive posture it is a truly impressive animal. The anterior two-fifths of its 10-foot (3-m) length is raised well above the elevation of the resting snake and curved in an S. From that posture the big snake (and it looks *really* big when it's about to bite you!) can make impressively long and accurate strikes.

Coloration: The giant bird snake is olive green dorsally. Old adults may be almost unicolored but juveniles and young adults are usually patterned with a series of broad dark bands. The belly is a clear sulphur yellow. The giant bird snake gets big, up to 10 feet (3 m) in length.

The common bird snake, *P. poecilonotus*, is a smaller and more variably colored species. Adults are of some shade of brown (rarely charcoal) and are weakly patterned with reddish or olive crossbands. Juveniles are a warm, light brown to olive brown, and are rather strongly marked with crossbands. The belly is cloudy. This bird snake attains a length of about 6½ feet (19.5 cm).

Common bird snakes attain a length of about 6½ feet (2 m).

aestivation: period of warm weather inactivity, often triggered by excessive heat or drought

aglyphous: having solid teeth

albino: lacking normal black pigment

allopatric: not occurring together, but often adjacent

ambient temperature: temperature of the surrounding environment

anal plate: large scute (or scutes) covering the snake's anus

anerythristic: lacking red pigment.

anterior: toward the front

anus: external opening of the cloaca; the vent.

arboreal: tree-dwelling.

brille: transparent scale or "spectacle" covering each eye of a snake.

brumation: the reptilian and amphibian equivalent of mammalian hibernation.

caudal: pertaining to the tail.

cb/cb: captive-bred, captive-born.

cb/ch: captive-bred, captive-hatched.

chorioallantois: gas-permeable membranous layer inside the shell of a reptile egg.

cloaca: common chamber into which digestive, urinary, and reproductive systems empty, and that itself opens exteriorly through the vent or anus.

constricting: wrapping tightly in coils and squeezing.

convergent evolution: evolution of two unrelated species as the result of environmental conditions.

crepuscular: active at dusk and/or dawn.

deposition: as used here, the laying of the eggs or birthing of young.

deposition site: spot chosen by the female to lay her eggs or have young.

dimorphic: difference in form, build, or coloration involving the same species; often sex-linked.

diurnal: active in the daytime.

dorsal: pertaining to the back; upper surface.

dorsolateral: pertaining to the upper sides.

dorsum: upper surface.

ecological niche: precise habitat utilized by a species.

ectothermic: cold-blooded.

endemic: confined to a specific region.

endothermic: warm-blooded.

erythristic: prevalence of red pigment.

form: identifiable species or subspecies.

fossorial: adapted for burrowing; a burrowing species.

genus: taxonomic classification of a group of species having similar characteristics. The genus falls between the next higher designation of "family" and the next lower designation of "species." Genera is the plural of genus. It is always capitalized when written.

glottis: opening of the windpipe.

gravid: reptilian equivalent of mammalian pregnancy.

gular: pertaining to the throat.

heliothermic: pertaining to a species that basks in the sun to thermoregulate.

hemipenes: dual copulatory organs of male lizards and snakes.

hemipenis: singular form of hemipenes.

herpetoculture: captive breeding of reptiles and amphibians.

herpetoculturist: one who indulges in herpetoculture.

herpetologist: one who indulges in herpetology.

herpetology: study (often scientifically oriented) of reptiles and amphibians.

hibernacula: winter dens.

hybrid: offspring resulting from the breeding of two species.

hydrate: to restore body moisture by drinking or absorption.

insular: as used here, island-dwelling.

intergrade: offspring resulting from the breeding of two subspecies, often occurring naturally in the wild.

Jacobson's organs: highly enervated olfactory pits in the palate of snakes and lizards.

juvenile: a young or immature specimen.

keel: a ridge (along the center of a scale).

labial: pertaining to the lips.

lateral: pertaining to the side.

leucistic: different from albinism, leucism is result of the lack of pigment in all chromatophores. Leucistic animals are often pure white and lack a pattern. The eyes of most examples are blue or black.

melanism: a profusion of black pigment.

mental: the scale at the tip of the lower lip.

middorsal: pertaining to the middle of the back.

midventral: pertaining to the center of the belly or abdomen.

monotypic: containing but one type.

nocturnal: active at night.

ocellus (plural, ocelli): a spot of color (eye-spot) encircled by another color.

ontogenetic: age-related (color and/or pattern) changes.

oviparous: reproducing by means of eggs that hatch after laying.

ovoviviparous: reproducing by means of shelled or membrane-contained eggs that hatch prior to, or at deposition.

photoperiod: daily/seasonally variable length of the hours of daylight.

poikilothermic: a species with no internal body temperature regulation; the old term was "cold-blooded."

postocular: to the rear of the eye.

prehensile: adapted for grasping.

premaxillary: bones at the front of the upper jaw.

prey imprinting: preferring prey of only a particular species and/or color.

race: a subspecies.

rostral: the (often modified) scale on the tip of the snout.

scute: scale.

species: a group of similar creatures that produce viable young when breeding. The taxonomic designation that falls beneath genus and above subspecies; abbreviation: "sp."

subspecies: subdivision of a species. A race that may differ slightly in color, size, scalation, or other criteria; abbreviation: "ssp."

sympatric: occurring together.

taxonomy: science of classification of plants and animals.

terrestrial: land-dwelling.

thermoreceptive: sensitive to heat.

thermoregulate: to regulate (body) temperature by choosing a warmer or cooler environment.

vent: external opening of the cloaca; the anus.

venter: underside of a creature; the belly.

ventral: pertaining to the undersurface or belly.

ventrolateral: pertaining to the sides of the venter (belly).

INFORMATION

Amateur Societies

Despite the fact that corn and rat snakes are among the most popular of reptiles, we know of no clubs or societies dedicated to them alone. However, among the members of most herpetological societies, there are usually at least one or two individuals who are interested in rat snakes.

You may learn of the existence of regional herpetological societies by asking biology teachers/professors, curators, or other workers at museums and nature centers, at pet stores, or by accessing *www.kingsnake.com* on the web.

Professional Herpetological Societies

Herpetologist's League
c/o Texas Natural Heritage Program
Texas Parks and Wildlife Department
4200 Smith School Road
Austin, TX 78744

Society for the Study of Amphibians
  and Reptiles
Department of Zoology
Miami University
Oxford, OH 45056

Magazines

Reptiles Magazine
P.O. Box 6050
Mission Viejo, CA 92690

Books

Arnold, E. N. and J. A. Burton. *A Field Guide to the Reptiles and Amphibians of Britain and Europe.* London: Collins, 1978.

Bartlett, Richard D. *In Search of Reptiles and Amphibians.* Leiden: E. J. Brill, 1988.

_____. *Digest for the Successful Terrarium.* Morris Plains, NJ: TetraPress, 1989.

Conant, Roger and Joseph T. Collins. *A Field Guide to Reptiles and Amphibians; Eastern and Central North America.* Boston: Houghton Mifflin, 1991.

Mehrtens, John M. *Living Snakes of the World in Color.* New York: Sterling Publications, 1987.

Pope, Clifford H. *The Reptiles of China.* New York: American Museum of Natural History, 1935.

Stebbins, Robert C. *A Field Guide to Western Reptiles and Amphibians.* Boston: Houghton Mifflin, 1985.

Staszko, Ray and Jerry G. Walls. *Rat Snakes: A Hobbyist's Guide to Elaphe and Kin.* Neptune, NJ: TFH, 1994.

Ruby freckles adorn this amelanistic corn snake.

Gonyosoma frenatus (not discussed in text) is a beautiful leaf green rat snake that is only now (2006) becoming readily available to hobbyists.

Wright, Albert H. and A. A. Wright. *Handbook of Snakes.* Vol. I. Ithaca, NY: Comstock, 1957.

Magazine Articles

Bartz, H. and V. Scheidt. "Care and Breeding of the Chinese Twin-Spotted Rat Snake, *Elaphe bimaculata.*" The Vivarium, 2(2):8–10, 1989.

Cranston, T. "Natural History and Captive Husbandry of the Western Green Rat Snake." The Vivarium 2(1):8–11, 29, 1989.

Dowling, Herndon G. A Taxonomic Study of the Rat Snakes, Genus *Elaphe fitzinger.* II.

The subspecies of *Elaphe flavirufa* (Cope), Ann Arbor, MI: U of MI, 1952.

____. A taxonomic study of the rat snakes, genus *Elaphe fitzinger.* V. The Rosaliae Section. Ann Arbor: U of MI, 1957.

____. A taxonomic study of the rat snakes. VI. Validation of the genera *Gonyosoma waglerand Elaphe fitzinger,* Copeia (1):29–40, 1958.

____. A taxonomic study of the rat snakes, genus *Elaphe fitzinger.* VII. The triaspis section. Zoologica 45:53–80, 1960.

INDEX

About the Authors

R. D. Bartlett is a herpetologist who has authored more than 600 articles and six books, and coauthored an additional 40 books. In 1970 he began the Reptilian Breeding and Research Institute, a private facility. Since its inception, more than 200 species of reptiles and amphibians have been bred at the RBRI, some for the first time in the United States under captive conditions. Bartlett is a member of numerous herpetological and conservation organizations, a cohost on an on-line reptile and amphibian forum, and a contributing editor of *Reptiles* magazine. Patricia Bartlett is a biologist and historian who has authored or coauthored 45 books on history and pet trade animals. A museum administrator, she has worked in both history and science museums. She serves in numerous local and state organizations.

Acknowledgments

As there is in any compilation of notes and materials, when a book such as this is written, personal input from others in the field is sought. Such was the case here. Bill Love (Blue Chameleon Ventures), Rob MacInnes of Glades Herp, Chris McQuade of Gulf Coast Reptiles, Lance Jarzynka, Cheryl Bott, Dan Scolaro, and Ben Siegel unhesitatingly provided photographic opportunities. Eric Thiss of Zoobook Sales, Bill Brant of The Gourmet Rodent, and Bruce Morgan allowed us to photograph many specimens. Jim Harding offered thoughts regarding fox snakes in Michigan, and Carl May shared his findings on anerythristic corn snakes in southern Florida. Information and thoughts on natural history and captive care were offered by Mike Souza (green rat snake), Bruce Morgan (various species), and Ernie Wagner (European rat snakes). And, as always, our editor, Pat Hunter, offered suggestions and support throughout this project. To all, our most sincere thanks.

Photo Credits

All photos © R. D. Bartlett except for the Persian rat snake on page 5, taken by Dan Scolaro.

All inquiries should be addressed to:
Barron's Educational Series, Inc.
250 Wireless Boulevard
Hauppauge, NY 11788
www.barronseduc.com

ISBN-13: 978-0-7641-3407-4
ISBN-10: 0-7641-3407-8

Library of Congress Catalog Card No. 2005058867

Library of Congress Cataloging-in-Publication Data
Bartlett, Richard D., 1938–
    Corn snakes and other rat snakes : a complete pet owner's manual : facts & advice on care and breeding / R. D. Bartlett and Patricia P. Bartlett.
        p. cm. — (A complete pet owner's manual)
    ISBN-13: 978-0-7641-3407-4
    ISBN-10: 0-7641-3407-8
    1. Rat snakes as pets. 2. Corn snakes as pets.
    I. Bartlett, Patricia Pope, 1949– II. Title.
    III. Series.

SF459.S5B37 2006
639.3'96—dc22   2005058867

Printed in China
9 8 7 6 5 4 3